The Carnival of Consciousness

Also by Ashish Dalela:

Semantic Atomism
Semantic Reasoning
The Journey of Perfection
Material and Spiritual Natures
Conceiving the Inconceivable
The Science of God
Time and Consciousness
Conceiving the Inconceivable
The Balanced Organization
The Yellow Pill
Cosmic Theogony
Emotion
Mystic Universe
Moral Materialism
Signs of Life
Uncommon Wisdom
Gödel's Mistake
Quantum Meaning
Sāṅkhya and Science
Is the Apple Really Red?
Six Causes

The Carnival of Consciousness

SHABDAVERSE
VOLUME 1

Ashish Dalela

The Carnival of Consciousness—SHABDAVERSE Volume 1
by Ashish Dalela

Published by Shabda Press
press.shabda.co
ISBN 978-93-85384-46-2
v1.3 03/2026

SHABDA
PRESS

Contents

Series Preface i

Consciousness Has a Gender 1

The Relational Nature of Consciousness 11

Is the Material World an Illusion or Reality? 21

Why Dreams Feel Just Like Waking 32

What is a Person? 38

The Self as the Basis for Science 51

The Soul is Moving and the Body is Not Moving 68

Matter Is Not Insentient 75

Consciousness Expands by Concentration 85

How Do You Know You Are Not Dreaming? 92

Free Will vs. Willpower 112

Reincarnation—The Most Essential Spiritual Truth 122

Jīva Falldown—Understanding Anādi 154

The Modern Consciousness Studies Misnomer 176

Can Neuroscience Study the Mind? 181

Does Consciousness Control Matter? 194

Series Preface

SHABDAVERSE is a series of article collections, organized by topics. The articles in these collections were originally published online on the SHABDA website over many years. A series of articles written from 2014 to 2019 were earlier published in chronological order under the series title *Western Questions Eastern Answers*. The SHABDAVERSE series organizes articles from 2019 to 2025 by categories, rather than dates. This is for multiple reasons—(a) there are enough articles in each category to produce collections organized by categories, (b) readers wanting to read topic-focused collections might find this approach more convenient and cohesive than the chronological one, and (c) the topic-focused approach allows us to make unique covers for each book, after all, in the ultimate analysis, a book is judged by its cover!

All these articles follow an interdisciplinary approach to every topic—everyday experience, empirical evidence, problems with different ideas advanced in the past and present, how ideas may have evolved historically, how certain issues were seen and understood differently across cultures, and with a solution to any and all related open and unsolved problems, which can be validated through ordinary experience, empirical evidence, and rational arguments. I often cite statements and ideas from Vedic texts, not to substantiate my claims, but to establish that my ideas are not new, and that I as the author of these articles don't claim authorship of the ideas. I only aim to present ancient ideas in a modern language, so that present audiences may understand and appreciate them based on what they already trust.

Pursuant to the science-religion divide created during European Enlightenment, we see two opposite approaches to the study of ancient texts—(a) the religious approach takes an ancient text as a divine revelation to be trusted on faith at best, and (b) the scientific approach, which rejects these texts as the personal opinion of dogmatic scribes, unprovable through or contradictory to the available evidence, and focuses on collecting evidence, followed by speculation to find an explanation that fits that evidence.

The Vedic tradition differs from both of these. Ancient texts have been preserved in a written form for thousands of years, but in every successive era, those texts were explained through commentaries. The texts and the commentaries were never merged. That trend continues today, and those who like to read ancient texts with explanations can do so. However, these explanations do not contrast their ideas with those in present-day sciences and religions, because the Vedic tradition was historically inward-looking, not outward-looking. By continuing the same trend, commentaries on Vedic texts appear to most people as different ideas, not better or true ideas, when contrasted to the ideas found in other worldviews. In fact, those ingrained in other worldviews consider Vedic texts primitive because the Vedic ideas don't match the ideas they have received through their culture and education. Therefore, the inward-looking historical trend of the Vedic texts is not adequate for the present time. For the present time, the Vedic tradition must become outward-looking, and contrast itself to the ideas of the other worldviews.

Therefore, in these articles, we—(a) sometimes we begin with unsolved problems created by prevalent ideas and theories and try to solve them using reasoning and evidence, and then connect the solution to the ideas in ancient texts, and (b) sometimes we begin with ideas and theories in ancient texts and show how they are relevant to the present time by showing how they solve unsolved or open problems.

I have seen with consternation a tendency among many authors to take ancient ideas, reformulate them in convenient ways, disconnect them from the sources from where these ideas were taken, and present these ideas as an author's original work. I think that this approach constitutes a theft, disrespectful to the teachers and texts from where ideas were taken. But more importantly, it filters the tradition of texts and teachers through the opinionated lens of the author who takes ideas without attribution, and closes the door for readers to go back to the tradition for more exploration in the future. Authors with such attitudes present themselves as prophets of original ideas, while masking the actual prophets.

I aim to show people of the present time a path to the Vedic tradition, not pretend to be a prophet of original ideas. Personally, I'm convinced that everything I have written about is a miniscule fraction of all that can be written, understood, or derived from the Vedic texts, and hopefully, future generations will do more of what I have tried to do. My primary goal is to dispel the myth that the Vedic texts are like the texts of other religions which have to be accepted on faith, rather than reason and observation. I call the dispelling of this myth, the *scientific study of Vedic texts*, pursuant to the common definition of science as truth based on reasoning and evidence, in contrast to a religion based on blind faith or belief.

Ashish Dalela

Consciousness Has a Gender

Three Kinds of Genders

Matter in the Vedic texts is also consciousness, although a different type of consciousness. This is of three types—God, soul, and matter. This article extends that discussion and identifies three genders associated with the three types of consciousness—masculine, feminine, and neutral.

God has a dominantly masculine gender; His Sakti has a dominantly feminine gender; and the soul has a dominantly neutral gender. These genders arise due to the differences in their desires. However, when the soul becomes subordinate to God, then it also develops a masculine desire and gender, and when the soul becomes subordinate to God's Sakti, then it also develops a feminine desire and gender. These genders are ultimately understood in terms of the differences in their desires. Generically, the soul can alternately be called *he*, *she*, or *it*.

Three Kinds of Desires

Let's begin by identifying three kinds of desires—*wanting*, *needing*, and *willing*. To illustrate by an example, we can say: "I want to eat", "I need to eat", and "I'm willing to eat". When we say, "I want to eat", it is suggested that I'm not hungry (i.e. I don't need to eat), but I still have a desire to taste. When we say, "I need to eat", it is implied that I'm hungry and I'm eating not for taste, but for survival. And if we say, "I'm willing to eat", it is understood that I'm not hungry (and hence I don't need to eat), and I'm not desiring tasty food (I don't want to eat); but if food is offered to me, then I will accept it.

Conversely, when we say that "I don't want to eat", it is suggested that I will not enjoy eating, although I may or may not be hungry, and if food is offered then I may or may not accept it. Similarly, when we say that "I don't need to eat", it is implied that I'm not hungry, although I may or may not have a desire to eat, and I may or may not be willing to accept food if it is offered. Finally, when we say that "I'm not willing to eat", it is understood that I won't accept food, although I may or may not need to eat, and I may or may not want to eat. Thus, negation of wanting, needing, and willing is not necessarily the negation of each of the three types of desires, but only the negation of one of them.

Consequently, when we say that "desire is absent", it may not necessarily mean that each of the wanting, needing, and willing are absent. It can also mean that one of wanting, needing, or willing is absent, but the other two are present. In the worst case, when willing and needing are absent, and everything else is rejected, there is still a desire, although it is present as a 'rejection' rather than 'acceptance'. Therefore, there is no conscious state without desire.

Desires are Treated as Genders

The *wanting* desire is considered masculine, the *needing* desire is considered feminine, and the *willing* desire is considered neutral. Let's take an example. A form of God, called Paramātma, advents into this world, and accompanies the soul. This form of God, however, doesn't enjoy and suffer in this world, because He is not *wanting* to be in the world, and His wants are never fulfilled or unfulfilled. He also doesn't *need* to be in the world because He is self-satisfied. However, to guide the soul through the material journey, God is *willing* to enter the world. Therefore, we say that Paramātma doesn't want to be in the world, and doesn't need to be in the world, but He is willing to be present. By accepting this willing state of desire, God renounces His masculine desire of wanting, and accepts a neutral position of willingness. He is still the Supreme Person, but because He accepts the desire like the soul, therefore, in one sense He is like a soul. These two souls are hence described as two birds sitting on a branch of a material tree.

God's original desire is *wanting*. God is also said to be self-satisfied, and that is sometimes incorrectly interpreted to mean that He has no wants. A self-satisfied state means that He has no *needs*. He doesn't need to eat, to sleep, to be with anyone. And yet, He *wants* to eat, sleep, and be with others. When God acts on His wants, but without a need and without accepting what others want, then He is Supreme.

The Sakti of God has the original desire of *needing*. This type of desire is considered feminine. The Sakti is incomplete without God because She needs God. Sakti is power, but the power needs to be used. Therefore, the Sakti is not 'inert' in the sense of dull matter which doesn't need to be used. The Sakti is also a person—a feminine person—but Her desire is that of needing rather than wanting. Due to this needing, the Sakti often agitates God— "I need you". Likewise, sometimes, God agitates His Sakti— "I want you". As a result, the Sakti is said to be 'dependent' on God, because Her need is God. And God is said to be independent of Sakti because He doesn't need Sakti, although He wants Her.

The original position of the soul is *willing*. The soul doesn't need to eat, sleep, or be with anyone. However, when the soul enters the material body, then it develops these needs, by the association with the material nature. The material energy is expanded from the needing desire; therefore, all our senses are inherently needy. The eyes need to see, the tongue needs to taste and talk, the ears need to hear. Since the senses are hungry, therefore, they influence the soul's willingness to become neediness.

Likewise, when the soul contacts matter, and it considers itself the enjoyer, then it develops the masculine desire of wanting—namely, I want to acquire, control, and enjoy the material world.

Liberation from matter is freedom from wanting and needing. Of course, we know that the body must be fed to keep it alive, and the body must sleep to prevent madness. However, these are bodily needs, not the soul's needs. When the soul learns to differentiate these two, then liberation is attained. In the liberated state, the wanting and needing desires are substituted by the *willing* desire.

This simply means that I don't want to eat, and I don't need to eat, but I'm willing to eat if some food is available.

This position of willingness is called *sama-darshan* when everything is perceived equally in this world. In short, if something is available, it is accepted. But if it is not available, then there is no hankering for it.

Free Will and Free Won't

One of the illusions of the material world is that we have *wants* and *needs* and free will is generally equated to wanting. Experiments in neuroscience, however, have shown that the brain has neural activity before consciousness indicates an acceptance. This idea is already well-known to anyone who practices meditation—the mind wanders everywhere, and the meditator must control the mind. The wandering mind is not due to the soul; it wanders automatically. But the soul can control the wandering. Hence, the soul is differentiated from the mind, and mind control is the ability to *accept* and *reject* the mind's wandering. In short, the soul either willingly accepts the mind's thoughts, or rejects them.

Owing to this fact, the idea of free will is modified into *free won't* which is a different way of saying that we don't have wants and needs, but we accept and reject the automatically created desires.

In short, the soul's position is not wanting or needing; it is simply being willing or unwilling to participate in the wanting and needing created by the body and the mind. The material desire can be wanting or needing, but the soul's desire is willing or unwilling. In general, material life means willing to accept the wanting and needing generated by the material body and the mind, as the soul's own wanting and needing. And liberated life means the rejection of the wanting and needing generated by the material energy.

Therefore, free will is not wanting or needing. It is only accepting and rejecting or willing and unwilling. This idea is called *sankalpa* and *vikalpa* of the mind. The former means "being with the possibility" and the latter means "being against the possibility". Thus, the body automatically generates the need for hunger, sex, sleep, and protection, and the soul must accept or reject that automatically generated need. Likewise, the mind automatically generates wants and we accept or reject them. Due to the soul's ability to reject, the mind and the senses can be controlled; but this acceptance and rejection is not wanting or needing. It is willing. A strong will means the ability to resist the temptations of the body and the mind. Strong will is not the determination for material achievements. It means the rejection of these inducements produced by the body and the mind.

Mind Control in Yoga Philosophy

The Yoga Sutra begins by the statement: *yogah chitta vritti nirodhah,* or the end of *chitta vritti* is yoga. The term *vritti* means 'modification', and *vrta* means a circle or boundary. The *chitta* is compared to an ocean, and the *vritti* in the *chitta* is like waves in the ocean. These waves are created when a boundary is imposed on the *chitta*. When a membrane is fastened around a circular frame to create a drum, an external force causes the membrane to vibrate. In the same way, to free the *chitta* of its vibrations, one must remove the boundaries in the *chitta*. These boundaries constitute the definition of the self, and when the self identifies with these boundaries, it creates an identity, such as "I am man", "I am young", "I am an Indian", etc. When these boundaries are imposed on the *chitta,* it automatically produces thoughts. For example, if I have the boundary of "I am Indian", then nationalistic thoughts automatically arise in the mind. Likewise, when the boundary is "I am a man", then thoughts about women are automatically created in the mind. These thoughts are vibrations of the *chitta,* like waves in the ocean. We can try to stop these vibrations, but the vibrations never truly end so long as the boundaries in *chitta* exist.

The liberation in the Yoga Sutra process is therefore one of removing all kinds of boundaries. The problem is that it is very hard to remove these boundaries as long there is a body, a social identity, etc. because as long as we live in this world, we tend to carry these identities. Therefore, the liberation by this process is generally expected to take thousands of years.

A simpler process for liberation was hence prescribed by Sri Chaitanya: *cheto darpan mārjanam*. Instead of trying to stop the vibrations in the *chitta*, try to clean the *chitta* and create new types of boundaries, which will then create new types of vibrations. This new type of boundary is also a definition of the self, but it is given in relation to God and His Sakti. When the *chitta* is thus modified, then thoughts about the Lord and His energy are automatically created just like materialistic wants and needs are created automatically when the *chitta* is not purified of its false identities. The novelty is that our acceptance of materialistic thoughts is bondage, and the acceptance of the thoughts in relation to the Lord and His Sakti are liberation.

Even in this liberated state, the soul's position doesn't change. It still is willing, rather than wanting or needing. However, when the *chitta* is modified to create an identity in relation to the Lord and His Sakti, then, the wanting and needing produced in the *chitta* is the wanting and needing of the Lord and His Sakti, and the soul simply accepts this wanting and needing. Due to this acceptance, the soul cannot say that this is what *I want*, or this is what *I need*. He simply says: This is what the Lord wants, and this is what the Lord's Sakti needs. The soul's position of willing or accepting doesn't change, but the wanting and needing that the soul accepts as its own desires, changes through the spiritual process.

Gender Change Through Spirituality

Thus, the soul is neutral gender, but depending on the thoughts in the *chitta*, it becomes either masculine or feminine. In the material world, the soul becomes masculine when it wants material things, and feminine when it needs material things. The desire of wanting is somewhat easier to control than the desire for needing, and therefore, the masculine gender is considered superior. But that superiority is relative to *renunciation* of the material world: it is easier to renounce wants than needs.

Similarly, in the spiritual world, the soul becomes masculine when it wants the Lord, and feminine when it needs the Lord. The position of needing the Lord is a more helpless and forceful condition than the position of wanting the Lord. As a result, the love of the feminine is considered superior to the love of the masculine. The inferiority of the feminine in this world becomes superiority in the spiritual world because the inferiority is relative to renunciation and the superiority is relative to attachment.

The Relation to Impersonalism

The impersonalist claims that the soul is always "it" and never "he" or "she", and that is partially correct in the sense that the soul is Brahman, which doesn't have a gender. It is also the constitutional position of the soul in the sense that the soul's desire is always *willing* rather than *wanting* or *needing*.

However, the soul is not the only type of consciousness; God and His Sakti are different kinds of consciousness, and they are the primary masculine and feminine. When the soul becomes subordinate to these genders, then "it" becomes "he" or "she". Even in the material world, the soul is not "he" or "she", but it comes under the control of a gendered material reality and becomes "he" or "she".

Therefore, the impersonalist argues that the genders in the spiritual world must be just like the genders in the material world, and if both genders are alien to the soul, then both must constitute a fallen condition. This latter idea is rejected in Vaishnava philosophy, after accepting that the soul is not truly the feminine or the masculine, although it becomes *subordinate* to the masculine or feminine, and by that subordination, it acquires the desires that exist in the original masculine and feminine.

The rejection of impersonalism (at this stage, which is again modified later, as we will see subsequently in the post) is therefore very subtle: (1) the soul is "it" and not "he" or "she" by itself, and (2) when the soul becomes subordinate to the masculine or feminine, then it becomes "he" or "she". This subordination is the willing of the soul—i.e. accepting the gender of "it", "he" or "she". Since the neutral gender is possible, therefore, impersonalism is not rejected in principle. However, it is rejected on the ground that the soul can accept a masculine or feminine desire spiritually.

The Rejection of Impersonalism

Impersonalism is ultimately rejected on the ground that there are three kinds of consciousness, which present themselves as masculine, feminine, and neutral genders. Hence, the philosophy of the soul cannot be extended to God and His Sakti; the soul can take on a neutral gender, but God and His Sakti are forever masculine and feminine. The soul can also take on a masculine or feminine gender because its desire is willing, and that willing can become subordinate to the wanting and needing.

Thus, all sorts of seemingly contradictory claims are reconciled. First, the soul enters a situation of bondage in the material world when it accepts a material gender. Second, the soul is superior to matter and it can reject the desires created by matter. Third, the soul can be free of qualities, including a gender, because it can exist as the neutral gender in Brahman. Fourth, the soul can accept all kinds of qualities, including a gender, as it becomes subordinate to the desires of the Lord and His Sakti.

As a result, you can say that (1) the material gender is false, (2) the soul has no spiritual gender, (3) the soul can accept a spiritual gender, and (4) the material gender can also be a spiritual gender. These contradictions cease to exist when the true nature of conscious desires is clearly understood.

If we insist that only Brahman is real, then we cannot explain how wanting and needing arise—even in the material world. We also cannot explain how the soul has wanting and needing, and yet is able to reject these things, because the wanting and needing must be innate to the soul because matter is already said to be inert. Only when we accept that the wanting and needing are separate from the willing, and yet, the willing can be subordinate to the wanting and needing, can we explain the material world. But when these two are accepted, then God and His Sakti are understood separately from the nature of the soul. As a result, we can also understand how the soul can take on new kinds of wanting and needing.

The difference between material and spiritual wanting and needing is also very subtle: the material desire is "I want" and "I need", whereas, the spiritual desire is "He wants" and "She needs". They can be confused only when "He" and "She" are dissolved, and everything becomes "I want" or "I need".

Innumerable Forms of Consciousness

Thus, in one sense, everything is consciousness. But in another sense, primarily there are three different kinds of consciousnesses, and they are differentiated by the nature of their desires. The masculine, feminine, and neutral archetypes are, however, not mutually exclusive. Rather, they mix incessantly to create innumerable forms of consciousness. Thus, some feminine forms can have masculine wants, although their primary desire is a feminine need. Likewise, some masculine forms can have feminine needs, although their primary desire is a masculine want. As a result, God is sometimes depicted in a masculine form, sometimes in a feminine form, and sometimes in an androgynous form.

The individuality of the conscious entity is then identified by the nature of desire. A different individual is also a different *type* of individual *personality*. As a result, it is now said that even the soul has a constitutional or "original" form, in the sense that it accepts a certain mixture of masculine wants and feminine needs as its own nature. Again, in one sense, the soul is neutral because it accepts and rejects, rather than wants or needs. And yet, it is masculine or feminine, because the desires it accepts or rejects can be masculine or feminine.

In the final analysis, each soul is a mixture of willing, wanting, and needing. But every soul is a different mixture of these three kinds of desires. As a result, each soul is an eternally unique individual. In the soul, however, the willing is always dominant, and therefore, the soul never attains the position of God or His Sakti. Likewise, in God and His Sakti, the wanting and needing are always dominant, so They never become the soul. Hence, in one sense, there is an absolute distinction between God, His Sakti, and the soul. In another sense, sometimes the soul can be almost on par with God or His Sakti, and God and His Sakti can almost seem to be like the soul. Likewise, in some situations, God can seem to be just like His Sakti, and vice versa.

To the novice, this can seem overwhelming, and hence a simple idea is presented: the soul is different from matter; the soul is Brahman, and matter is illusion. But this simplistic view proves problematic on closer inspection, and the doctrine is updated to address the issues with the simplistic doctrine. These enhancements are for the advanced students, not for the novices. If one is not detached from material life and starts considering their material desire as their spiritual desire, then the result would always be a disaster. Therefore, deeper philosophical expositions are also necessary for the removal of misunderstandings.

The Relational Nature of Consciousness

Introduction and Overview

Vedic texts describe the self in three words, namely, *sat*, *chit*, and *ānanda*. The chit is the knower and known, sat is knowing, and ānanda is the happiness derived from the knower knowing the known. What we call 'consciousness' is the process of knowing that operates under the knower's happiness. We can also use the terms 'relation', 'cognition, and 'emotion' to describe these three aspects. The enjoyer is the emotion, the enjoyed is the cognition, and the enjoying is their mutual relation. Then, what we call 'consciousness' is the relationship between the knower and the known. I will use this article to delve into the different kinds of relations. The study of these relationships constitutes the "science" of consciousness.

The Problem of Material Reduction

The modern "scientific" study of consciousness is a euphemism for trying to explain consciousness based on some material objects and their forces. The problem is that the force of an object acts on other objects rather than on itself. If knowledge is the byproduct of force, then to know oneself, and call that "I", the force of an object must act on itself. Since all forces tend to push or pull something else, therefore, when a force acts on itself, it must push or pull itself. This self-acting force will now cause something to move by itself. If the self-acting force causes something to accelerate or decelerate, then it will gain or lose energy and the law of conservation of energy would be falsified.

This problem is encountered while speaking about self-acting forces in gravitation. For instance, if different parts of a galaxy pull themselves toward each other, then it will cause the galaxy to collapse onto itself. As the galaxy begins shrinking, the mass gets more concentrated and the distance between masses begins to reduce. The result of shrinking distances and concentrating masses is an increasing gravitational force which accelerates the pace of shrinking and concentrating. Ultimately, either the total mass is still the same but the total energy has become infinite, or the energy transforms into mass and we get infinite mass with the same energy, or both mass and energy become infinite.

If we uphold the conservation of energy, then the law of gravitational force must be voided at small distances. Otherwise, if law of gravitational force is upheld, then the law of conservation of energy must be voided. Both laws cannot be true simultaneously. Self-force creates a contradiction between two laws such that only one of the two laws could be true. Thereby, of self-action causes the laws of this action to break down. This is then the problem of materialist reduction of consciousness: It can either be inconsistent or incomplete.

An Alternative Science of Consciousness

Vedic philosophy doesn't think in this way. When the self wants to know itself, a picture of the self is manifest from the self, consciousness connects to this picture, and the picture is then reflected back into consciousness. However, since that picture was previously produced from the self, therefore, reflection of the picture within the self isn't the *addition* of anything new. It is simply the recognition and realization of what was already in the self. When the self produces a picture of the self, the self is not reduced. When the picture is reflected back into the self, the self is not increased. The self remains the self, and yet, it acquires knowledge of itself without the self becoming infinite.

In the alternative science of consciousness, reality is modeled as mind and thought rather than as object and force. The object and force model results in infinities. But the mind and thought model does not. This alternative is succinctly summarized in the

Īśopaniṣad as follows: "That is complete, this is complete, from the complete comes the complete, but after removing the complete from the complete, the balance is complete." We can understand this in terms of mind and thought. The mind is the first complete. It manifests a picture of itself, which is the second complete. After manifesting the picture, the self remains complete. If the picture merges back into the self, then the second complete disappears but the first complete does not increase. If the two completes are called "energy", then "energy" neither increases nor decreases.

We can do a consistent and complete science of consciousness with this model, and then we can extend it to study matter. In that science, there is a center of a galaxy which is a knower. The expanse of the galaxy is a picture of the self manifest from the knower to become a known. If the galaxy collapses on itself, then known picture collapses back into the self, without producing an infinity. If the galaxy then explodes, it is just the self expanding itself into a picture of the self to become the known. The galaxy and the universe can thereby expand, to create an ever-increasing detailed picture of the self, without decreasing energy. The same galaxy and the universe can also collapse, to create an ever-decreasing abstract picture of the self, without increasing energy. The expanding or collapsing universe now becomes a self expanding from itself or collapsing into itself. Neither presents a paradox. Hence the model of mind and thought remains consistent and complete.

The Description of Reality as Knowledge

All over Vedic texts, we find the whole of reality being described as Jñāna or knowledge. This knowledge can be divided into three parts, namely, the knower, the known, and the knowing. These three parts can also be merged back into knowledge. The knowledge can also be summarized or detailed. If summarized knowledge is detailed, then the summarized knower, known, and knowing expands into multiple knowers, knowns, and knowings. If detailed knowledge is summarized, then multiple knowers, knowns, and knowings collapsed into one knower, known, and knowing.

The fact that they prior existed as part of 'knowledge' is *oneness* or non-differentiated nature called Param-Brahman. But since they have separated, there are numerous knowers, knowns, and relationships of knowing. However, these separated knowers, knowns, and knowings are not truly separable from the original knower just like a thought cannot be separated from the thinker. At the point of thinking, the thought seems separate from the thinker. However, that is just appearance rather than reality. The separation exists as phenomena and non-separation exists as reality.

Once knowledge has divided into many knowers, knowns, and knowings, each knower can know infinite other knowns through the relation of knowing. Each knower can also produce more knowns from itself, just like a mind manifests thoughts. Finally, some knowns can collapse back into the knower just like thoughts merge back into the thinker. The merged thought hasn't disappeared. The expanded thought hasn't appeared. They are all eternally real. However, they are manifest or unmanifest. The technical Sanskrit terms are *vyakta* and *avyakta* respectively.

Self-Awareness and World-Awareness

I will devote the rest of this article to the relationships of knowing. Let's start with the intuition about observations. Suppose you are observing an apple. The apple is the known, you are the knower, and what we call 'consciousness' is the relation between the two. In this relationship, there is always *aboutness*—we say that my experience is *about* the apple. This aboutness (Franz Brentano called this 'intentionality') creates the simultaneous sense in which you and the apple are distinct (i.e., real) and yet inseparable (as part of knowledge). The existence of 'knowledge' requires that there be a knower, a known, and a knowing. Since this knowledge exists, therefore, we cannot separate the knower, the known, and the knowing. And yet, despite this inseparability, we cannot equate the knower to the known to the knowing.

Thus, consciousness creates a relation between the knower and the known, and these relations come in many varieties. One such relation is that of self-awareness, in which the knower, the known, and the knowing are the same thing, and this process can be understood if we say that there is knowledge of the self, but it is comprised of three aspects—the knower, the known, and the knowing.

Thus, *sat*, *chit*, and *ānanda* are three components of self-awareness. Similarly, when we are aware of an apple, then the knower, the known, and the knowing still exist, but they are not the same thing; you are the knower, the apple is the known, and the relation between the two is knowing.

In this way, we can describe both self-consciousness and world-consciousness by the same three principles. And this means that if we study the world as experience or observation, then the theory of world-experience can also be used to understand self-experience, or the "I-ness". As a result, separate theories for the soul and matter are not needed, if we have the correct theory of experience.

Scientific Modeling of Relationships

Let us now briefly turn to how relationships can be modeled in science. Modern mathematics models these relationships as *functions*. In set theory, these functions are classified into three broad categories, called *injective*, *surjective*, and *bijective* relationships. A relation R: A → B is called *injective* if every element of B has *at most* one corresponding element in A. Similarly, a relation R: A → B is called *surjective* if every element of B has *at least* one corresponding element in A. If a relation is both injective and surjective, then every element in B has one and only one corresponding element in A, and it is called *bijective*. Typically, an injective relation entails that B is *bigger* than A. A surjective relation means that A is *bigger* than B. And a bijective relationship means that both of these sets are equal-sized.

Vedic philosophy replaces big, small, and equal, with *superior*, *inferior* and *equal*. The notions of big and small are quantitative, and the notions of inferior and superior are qualitative. A relationship of superiority S: A → B means that A is superior to B. A exerts control over B, therefore, in some sense, it is 'bigger' than B. And yet, it is not physical bigness that we are talking about. Likewise, a relationship of inferiority I: A → B means that A is inferior to B. B exerts control over A, therefore, in some sense, it is 'bigger' than A. The relationship of equality E: A ↔ B means that A and B exert control over each other, so they are not superior or inferior to each other.

Different Classes of Relationships

Now, let's consider some examples. The relation of superiority exists in the parent-child and boss-subordinate interactions. The parent is in control of the child, and the boss is in control of the subordinate. Therefore, when they are conscious of the other thing, the consciousness is also of being a parent or a boss. As a result, we now no longer describe consciousness merely as some 'awareness' but in terms of a *type*. The relation of inferiority can be grasped by seeing the same thing from the perspective of the child or the subordinate.

The relationship of equality is seen between friends; they can control each other, so they are not mutually superior or inferior. Therefore, we say that friendship is a relation of equality. It is also a bidirectional relationship, similar to the *bijective* relations between two sets.

Mistaking Equality as Identity

This sense of 'equality' leads to a problem if the equality is interpreted as *identity*. In the case of knower and known, a sense of equality can lead to the knower *identifying* itself with the known. We can call this the *identity relation,* in which two things that are equal to each other are considered to be *identical* to each other.

This relation appears when the soul perceives the body and then finding that everything in the soul can exist in the body, and everything in the body can exist in the soul, sees a relationship of equality. Very quickly, however, this equality relation becomes the *identity relation* and we start saying that "I am the body", "I am in love", "I am in pain", "I am a man", "I am a woman", "I am hurt", "I am old", "I am young", "I am rich", "I am poor", and so on.

Each of these is an attribute of the body. The soul is observing this body quite like the body is observing the apple. But while observing the apple, the relationship is that of superiority—"I can control, own, eat, or throw the apple". However, while observing the body, the relationship is that of equality. The relation between body and soul is quite like a *bijective relationship* but it is not *identity*. There are indeed two separate things—the body and the soul—which have a one-to-one bijective relationship. However, when the bijective relationship is misinterpreted as the identity relation, then the illusion of the soul being the body arises.

Factually, the soul also has a bijective relationship to itself, and this bijective relation is also the identity relation, in the sense that there is the knower, the known, and the knowing, and these are the aspects of the same thing—the soul. Hence, there is a basis for converting the bijective relation to an identity relation, and that basis exists in the case of self-awareness. If that identity relation is mistakenly applied to the body, then the soul identifies with the body, as *equality is interpreted as identity*.

Theory of Bondage and Liberation

The process of liberation is freedom from this illusion, and it means that we look upon the body like the body sees the apple. This is the relation of *superiority* in which I am in control of the body. This liberated soul stops identifying with the body and gains control over it.

If the soul identifies with the body, it comes under the *inferiority* relationship in which the body demands food and the soul says "I am hungry"; the body demands sleep, and the soul says "I am sleepy". Thus, the process of material entanglement involves the conversion of the superiority relation to a relationship of equality, which then becomes the inferiority relation, and by identifying with the body, the body gains complete control over the soul. Now, the materialist, under this inferiority relationship says: There is nothing other than the body.

The process of liberation is therefore very simple, and yet subtle: (1) I am not controlled by the body, (2) I am not identical to the body, and (3) I am the controller of this body. We transform the relationship between soul and body from inferiority and equality to the relationship of superiority. In that condition, we have an identity relation to the self, and this process is called *self-realization*.

Three Types of Consciousness

The idea that we are controlled by the body is called 'materialism'.

The idea that I am identical to the body (and there is no soul apart from the body) is called Buddhism. And the idea that I am identical to myself, and nothing else exists (other than the self) is called self-realization.

Thus, just based on the ideas of superiority, inferiority, and equality we can identify three kinds of consciousness—the materialist consciousness, the voidism consciousness, and the self-consciousness.

The materialist says that there is indeed consciousness, but it is *produced* from the body, or that consciousness is an effect or epiphenomena of material interactions. The voidist says that there is no such thing as body and consciousness; there is just conscious experience and we call that the body. The materialist is a realist, while the voidist is an idealist. In materialism, if you stop experiencing, the world still exists. In voidism, the end of the experience is the end of the world. Therefore, the voidist tries to end experience, which is called the end of reality.

The "Neither" Type of Consciousness

Vedic philosophy goes beyond these three states and identifies two more types of consciousness, which are paradoxical in nature.

The first type of consciousness is that which constitutes the *neither* superior, *nor* inferior, *nor* equal relationship. This relation is sometimes called *śānta* or "silent appreciation". For example, the liberated soul, after gaining self-awareness and distinction from the body, directs its awareness toward God—the source of everything. He doesn't consider himself equal to God, or inferior to God, or superior to God. He merely acknowledges the existence of God as the source of everything. Just as a fan might appreciate a great person, without saying that I'm equal to that person, that I'm a subordinate to that person, or I am superior to that person, similarly, in this state, God's existence is recognized, somewhat dispassionately. This recognition of God—from a distance, and silently—constitutes the Brahman realization.

Then there are many other types of relationships that vary upon the neither superior, nor inferior, nor equal relationships, but they are not as distant as the silent appreciation. We can compare these to the relationships between citizens, neighbors, colleagues, and distant relatives.

For example, the *sālokya* liberation is just like the affection between two citizens, but living far off. The *sāmipya* liberation is like being neighbors. The *sārsti* liberation is just like being professional colleagues. And the *sārupya* liberation is just like being distant relatives. In these relations, there is more affection than silent appreciation. But there is an absence of intimate relationships like those of lovers, friends, parents, or servants. Finally, there is also a relationship of equality which is *confused as identity*. In this relation, the soul merges into God and loses its identity. This is called the *sāyujya-mukti*. All these types of relationships are considered *mukti* or liberation from matter.

The "Both" Type of Consciousness

Then, there is a second type of paradoxical consciousness, which is simultaneously superior, inferior, and equal. This kind of relationship is one of romantic love between the Lord and His devotees. The lovers control each other, the lovers are controlled by each other, and the lovers are equal to each other. So, each lover is superior, inferior, and equal, and they are simultaneously superior, inferior, and equal.

Apart from this, there are relationships of superiority, inferiority, and equality, in which the simultaneity of the previous (romantic love) is absent. These are pure relations of superiority, inferiority, and equality. The relationship of superiority makes the soul a parent of the Lord. The relationship of inferiority makes the soul a servant of the Lord. And the relationship of equality makes the soul a friend of the Lord.

What is the Science of Consciousness?

Thus, immense variety in relationships is created from the basic three types of relationships as superior, inferior, and equal. The study of this variety is the "science" of consciousness. A true "theory" of consciousness requires a discussion of superior, inferior, and equal relationships which are about control rather than merely size or quantity, as the relations of injection, surjection, and bijection are in mathematics.

Unlike the physical and quantitative relationships of mathematics, the qualitative relationships create *roles* of lovers, parent-child, master-servant, friend, colleague, neighbor, distant fan, citizen, etc. Each role creates patterns of acceptable and unacceptable behaviors. In the material world, the concept of *duty* (or *dharma*) arises from the roles, which depend on the relationships. When someone indulges in unacceptable behaviors, there is *karma*, and the laws of nature then change the relationships—e.g., put us from a position of power and control, into a relationship where we lose the power of control. Thus, the description of relationships, roles, duties, and laws of behavior form a continuum of a new kind of science that lies beyond modern science, but it can be rational based on everyone's experience of these phenomena.

Is the Material World an Illusion or Reality?

The Doctrine of Māyāvāda

All over Vedic texts, the material nature or prakriti is also termed as māyā, which literally means—"that which is not". Pursuant to this, there is a doctrine called Māyāvāda, which says that the world doesn't exist. It is literally like a "hallucination", which has no objective reality—independent of the observer.

But if that were the case, then why would two people have the *same* hallucination? For example, if you were looking at a building alongside your friend, and you agree that there is indeed a building, then what would be the reason for that agreement? To be fully consistent, the Māyāvāda doctrine now says that there isn't actually a friend "out there". Rather, what we call a "friend" is also a construct within our consciousness—quite like the building you see. Indeed, the other person is also a hallucinatory construct in which two individual personalities are created as an effect of māyā. Therefore, it is not just the building that is hallucinatory, but even the individuality of different persons that is a hallucination.

The Māyāvāda position can be further extended to say that when we talk to another person, and he seems to respond, that question and the answer are both the creation of māyā—i.e., a hallucination. In reality, there is just one consciousness, which when covered by māyā creates the notion of many individual persons and many individual things. Even if God appeared in your vision, that vision would also be a hallucination. The only thing that we can be sure of is that there is *one* consciousness.

This position is slightly more sophisticated than solipsism in Western philosophy where only I exist, and the world is merely an image in my consciousness. The sophistication is that now, even "I" doesn't exist; it is as much a creation of māyā as the "other". This sophistication allows us to solve the problem of realism in a new way—we can say that there are many "I" created due to māyā and the consciousness is itself divided into many "I". To support this argument, the Māyāvāda doctrine gives the example of space, and how it is seen from within a pot. Space itself is called Mahākāsha, while the space from within the pot is called Ghatākāsh. The argument is that whatever consciousness we have in this body is not the real consciousness; it is rather the consciousness that has already been put into a 'pot'. Thereby, it has been divided into potted spaces, but if you break all the pots, then space is only one.

It is almost impossible to defeat Māyāvāda because the philosophy is completely self-consistent, with one practical issue. That issue is that if all "embodied consciousness" is an illusion, then one cannot be considered liberated unless this "pot" of the body and mind is broken. Since that potted nature exists until we are dead, there is no way to know if someone is self-realized until they are dead. But when they are dead, there is no way to know if they were transcendental anyway. So, while in theory, the doctrine is self-consistent, there is no practical way of knowing if someone has transcended the world or not because the only way to know that is after their death. To counteract this problem, the concept of jīvana-mukta was created in Vedic philosophy—a person who is liberated *even* in this body.

If someone can be liberated even while living in the body, then the body cannot be called the cause of bondage. Likewise, that liberated stage would entail that the individuality of the soul is not due to māyā. So, now, the criticism of Māyāvāda reduces to just one argument—namely, that liberation in this body is possible. That liberated stage allows us to select the guru, who can then liberate others. That liberated stage becomes the foundation on which *all* the contentions of Māyāvāda—namely, the claim that there is only one consciousness, that the world is an illusion, that even vision of God is an illusion—are rejected. Since this entire doctrine rests on the concept of jīvana-mukta, unless a person is truly liberated in this body, there can always be shades of Māyāvāda in their philosophy. The Māyāvāda philosophy is very easy to understand and very hard to disprove, and hence it remains very popular.

The Doctrine of Māyā

However, once we reject Māyāvāda, we are still left with numerous statements about māyā in the Vedic texts. What do we do with them? We cannot reject māyā along with Māyāvāda, because that would undermine the entire Vedic system of philosophy. Therefore, the claim that the material world is māyā must be accepted, but it must be *understood* in a new way. In short, it is not enough that you reject Māyāvāda *unless* you can provide a new interpretation of māyā. Unless an alternative understanding of māyā is presented, the criticism of Māyāvāda is tantamount to rejecting the entire Vedic system.

This alternative understanding of māyā, however, is so subtle and nuanced that people find it very hard to accept it. But without this alternative view of māyā, there is no other criticism of Māyāvāda. So, despite the difficulties in this alternative view of māyā, it must be accepted, even if it seems hard.

The alternative view of māyā is that the world is like a book, comprised of text. The text has three properties—(a) of its existence, (b) of its meaning, and (c) of its truth. The term 'māyā' pertains to the fact that the text exists, it is meaningful, but it is *not* true. Let's illustrate this idea with an example.

Suppose a man says to a woman "I love you". Under Māyāvāda, this statement was never truly uttered; we just hallucinated that such a statement was said. But under the alternative view of māyā, the statement was uttered, and it was meaningful, but it was not true. The claim that the world is māyā, therefore, amounts to saying that the world is a collection of *false* claims. Yes, they are uttered, and they are meaningful. But because they are false, they cannot be *trusted*. Conversely, if the same statement "I love you" is uttered in the spiritual world, then it exists, it is meaningful, and it is true. The difference between matter and spirit is therefore extremely subtle. Both worlds exist. Both worlds comprise things that are meaningful. But one world is true claims and the other is false claims.

But What Is Truth?

This description of māyā doesn't quickly abate the problem, because we must now define what we mean by *truth*. A simple definition of truth is called the *Correspondence Theory of Truth* and it says that a statement is true *if* it corresponds to reality. But the "reality" in question is not an easily understood thing. For example, if you say "I love you" the reality would be determined by whether you truly feel the love, or you are faking it. To decide if "I love you" is true, we must delve into a person's mind.

Now, we must recall that the so-called reality is also a statement or text. So the correspondence notion of truth comes down to the *consistency* between two sentences—the first sentence is reality and the second sentence is the statement about that reality. This creates a big problem because if your feeling of love is another sentence, then how do we know that *that* statement is indeed true? Obviously, we will need another statement to which that statement must be consistent. Vedic philosophy answers this problem in a curious way. It says that there are indeed many *levels* of statements.

For example, giving a person gifts is a superficial statement of love, which can be taken as the evidence for the truth of "I love you". So, if a person says "I love you" and then gives someone a gift, one can say that the statement "I love you" was true. But this doesn't establish the truth with certainty, because someone may give a gift, but only with the intent of cheating the person at a later time. To solve this problem, we have to go slightly deeper—e.g., into the mental state. Is a person truly feeling the feelings of love while giving gifts and saying "I love you"? But what happens when they are feeling the love right now but will stop feeling the love later? How do we know that they are truly in love, not merely saying so due to feelings of lust? To solve this problem, we have to go to an even deeper level into their belief system, because differences of beliefs can lead to clashes subsequently, and that would then destroy their love. Once the compatibility between these beliefs is established, then we ask: Do they have the same goals? This is because differences of goals—even if they have the same beliefs—can destroy love. Then, if they have the same goals, we must go to an even deeper level of their value system, because differences in values crop up over a much longer period of time, and can destroy the love. Ultimately, when we cross all these thresholds, we must ask the most fundamental question: Is the person selfish or unselfish? Is the person prepared to make the sacrifices over time—no matter how big those sacrifices are? Or are they going to say at some point in time: "This is too much for me, and I cannot sacrifice everything eternally".

In this way, the truth of "I love you" is a very complicated problem, because whatever seems to be real may not truly be *consistent* with a deeper reality, and hence not *true*. It can be said to exist and can be said to be meaningful, but because it disappears, it is not *true*. Thus, this process of deciding truth is simplified into a single conclusion: *Whatever is true must be eternal.*

Since everything in the material world is temporary, therefore, none of it is true. Yes, it exists for the moment. Yes, it is meaningful for the moment. But it is not true. Hence, the world is māyā.

Now, if you are feeling delighted at this conclusion of "truth is eternity", save it for the moment. Because Māyāvāda has the same conclusion. Māyāvāda also says that the material world is an illusion because it is temporary, and Brahman is eternal, and therefore, it is the *only* truth. Therefore, whatever complicated reasoning for establishing the truth we went through before, can also be co-opted by the Māyāvāda philosophy, and lead to the same conclusion—i.e., the world doesn't exist. You might say that the world exists but is false in its claims, and the Māyāvāda philosopher can say that it doesn't exist because it is not true, and that subtlety of distinction would be totally immaterial and irrelevant because the ultimate conclusion in both cases that the material world is māyā because it is temporary.

All Temporary Things are Not False

Now, to salvage the situation, we have to make an even deeper point, namely, that *some* temporary things are *true*. For example, if there is a book on true knowledge, it may not be eternal. The book may exist for some time, and then go out of publication, all the copies of the book may be destroyed over time, and the knowledge would cease to exist. Since that book ceases to exist, by the previous conclusion that "truth is eternal", this book on true knowledge would also become false.

The solution to this problem is obviously that some temporary things are also true. Now, this is a big problem, because we earlier said that "whatever is true is eternal". If we simply negate this statement, then we will get "all that is temporary is also false", but we are not prepared to accept that. So, we need two seemingly contradictory statements: (a) truth is eternal, and (b) temporary can also be true.

How do we reconcile this conundrum? The answer is that we can do so *if* we draw a distinction between existence, meaning, and truth. The book's existence can be temporary, but its meaning can be eternally true. Conversely, some books—e.g., books on fiction—can also have a temporary existence, and their meanings are eternally false. Then, some books—e.g., on political facts of a nation—can have a temporary existence, and their meanings can be temporarily true. So, now, when someone says that the world is temporary, we can agree. But we can disagree with the claim that everything in the world is false since falsity or māyā is about the truth of the meaning, not merely the temporality. Accordingly, there can be things that are never true, sometimes true, and always true. This truth pertains to the *meaning* and not to the *existence*. Thus, if the Vedas ceased to exist, their knowledge doesn't become false. It can still be eternal truth because the truth pertains not to existence but *only* to the meaning.

The Radical Shift in Discourse

Thus, when we say that "truth is eternal" we don't mean that it exists in this world eternally. It can appear or disappear, and if it disappears, then God and His devotees establish it again. But from the perspective of this world, the truth *appears* temporarily, even though it *exists* eternally. Thus, we draw a distinction between *material existence* (which is temporary) and *spiritual existence* (which is eternal).

But what is existence? Why does something that exists eternally only *appear* temporarily? This is when we have to say that all individual things are a combination of two things—concepts and individuality. An individual table for instance is the combination of an idea (table) and an individuality. When the idea combines with the individuality, then the table appears (temporarily). But when the idea separates from the individual, then the table disappears. This is very radical because now the individual tables and chairs are *not physical things*; they are actually symbols of meaning—an idea and its instantiation.

Therefore, tables can also exist in the spiritual world, and hence they can be eternally true. And yet, tables exist in this world, and they are temporary. They are both 'tables'—the idea is the same. But one is temporary and the other is eternal because the individual and idea combination is temporary or permanent. A good example of this fact is the installation of a deity. The form of the deity is an idea, which has an eternal individual combined to the form in the spiritual world. When we form a deity out of a stone, then the same form exists in this world, although it has been instantiated temporarily. That temporary instance is the temporary advent of God in this world. Therefore, if you break the deity, you haven't destroyed God. But if you worship the deity, then you are directly worshiping God.

If the material world was wholly an illusion, God's deity would also be an illusion (this is indeed the position of Māyāvāda). But the nuanced understanding of māyā is that the material world is temporary and not *completely* false. There is also truth in this world—e.g., scriptures and deities are true. And their truth depends on the meaning of these things being true. That meaning in turn depends on a deeper meaning being true, and so on, until the deepest level meaning—which is self-evident—is true.

The radical shift in thinking is that what we call 'matter' is just temporary instantiation of temporary or eternal meaning, while what we call 'spirit' is the eternal instantiation of eternal meaning. It is not "stuff" or "substance". If it were stuff or substance, then all of it would be temporary, and whatever is temporary would be considered false. If this whole world is false, then you can never *know* the truth because books on truth could never be considered true—after all, these books are temporary.

So, the mere existence of true knowledge requires many things:

(1) truth is about ideas, not about existence, (2) all existents must be instances of ideas, and (3) ideas can be temporary or eternal. Now, when you study the material world, you must think of everything as the instance of an idea. That instance is not important; the idea that the instance symbolizes is the most important thing.

The Material World is Text

All these conclusions are presented in Vedic philosophy in different forms. For example, the material world emanates from śabda-brahman, which is a primordial form of language; the world is just like books or texts created from language. Likewise, what we call 'space' has the property of sound with meaning; the meaning is in the mind, and the sound is the instance of meaning. So, when you see a table or a chair, it is not "stuff". It is rather alphabets, words, and sentences that encode a description. When we perceive this description by our senses (which are also text), then an experience is created. Similarly, we can say that our experience is 'meaning' and the external reality is the 'words'. The words are produced from meanings, and the meaning can be grasped from the words. Reality is text.

Now, what we call "space" is not the space of "stuff". It is rather the space of meanings. Two things that are close in this space have similar meanings; the things that are far in this space have dissimilar meanings. Based on this, when two planets are far-off, it is because they are different meanings. When two planets are close, then they are similar meanings. This "semantic space" is not *physical space*. A new sense of distance and proximity is required to even understand proximity and distance.

With this, you can throw all of the modern science out of the window. There is nothing called energy, mass, charge, momentum, etc. There is only text. There are no laws such as gravitation or electromagnetism; there are laws of meaning—e.g., new meaning is created by the combination of words. There is simply no determinism—because the combination of letters into words or sentences is based on a choice. When you make a combination, your choices must be responsible, so there is a law of karma. Thus, an alternative science of matter emerges, based on the idea that it is not *things*; it is rather *text*.

Māyā and God

So, what is māyā? It is the ability to create false stories as the worldly text. Not all text is false, however. The term māyā simply denotes all the text whose meanings are false. The text exists, although temporarily (just as the true text is temporary). The text is always meaningful (otherwise it would not be considered text). So, you cannot distinguish between reality and falsity based on existence or meaning. You must rather distinguish based upon the *truth* of the meaning. That truth requires the truth of a deeper meaning, which depends on the truth of even deeper meaning, and so on. If any of these truth conditions break down, then the whole thing is false, and hence it can be called māyā.

Thus, the simple conclusion of Vedic texts is that all that is connected to God—i.e., based on the truth in God—is also true. And whatever negates any of the many levels of reality connected to God is māyā. If any of the truths emanated from God are *negated,* that negation of the truth is māyā. That negation also exists—for example, we can say that "sky is not blue" and the sentence exists. But you cannot say that it is true merely because it exists. You have to trace its connection to the deepest truth—God. In this way, God is truth, and māyā is simply the negation of that truth, which also *exists* but is *false.*

Thus, when God appears in this world, that form of God is *not* māyā, because it is not the negation of God. Likewise, when books about God are written, they are not māyā, even if they are temporary. And the jīvana-mukta person, who is devoted to God, is not māyā, even though he has a short lifespan. The deity of the Lord is not māyā, even though it appears and disappears at a certain point in time. Establishing the above truths itself requires changing our conception of matter completely.

The External and Internal Energies

In the book Six Causes, this notion of māyā is discussed at length, and māyā is described to be the *negation* of God. God is the original truth, and He expands into many subsidiary truths. One of these expansions is what God is *not*. And then there are many subsidiary expansions of what God is not. The expansions of truth are expanded from God's *pleasure*, and the expansions of falsity are produced from God's *austerity*. The Mahā Viṣṇu form of God creates the material world by performing austerities, or *tapasya*. Thus, He is not happy creating the world, and yet, an austerity is also a form of enjoyment.

The world that is created from austerity is called the "external energy" of God. Why is it external? It is so because it is what God is *not*. This negation of God is thus also called māyā, or that which is not (God). Likewise, the world that is created from pleasure is called the "internal energy" of God. Why is it internal? It is so because it is what God *is*. And yet, this world is also called *yoga-māyā* which perplexes many people: Is it also an illusion? The answer is yes and no. God has no father or mother, but He has the desire for a father and a mother; to fulfill this desire, the "illusion" of a father and a mother is created. Likewise, God has no brother or sister, but He has the desire for a brother and a sister; so, to fulfill this desire, a brother and a sister are manifest. God has no equal, but He has the desire for friendships; so, to fulfill this desire, many friends of God are manifest. They are all "illusion" but they are also real.

In what sense are they real? The answer is that they create greater happiness. When the illusion is happier, then it is considered truth—provided that illusion is *eternal*. So, at some point in philosophy, we defer the considerations of truth to whatever creates greater and eternal happiness. If illusion creates greater happiness, then it is also the greater truth! But we come to this point *after* rejecting material illusion because it is not only illusory but also temporary. Eternal illusion, if it is happier, it is also truer.

Māyā vs. Māyāvāda

In this way, the refutation of Māyāvāda requires a sophisticated understanding of what we mean by māyā, the textual or symbolic nature of the material world, the distinction between existence, meaning, and truth in these symbols, and the differences between the eternality of existence, meaning, and truth.

If this sophisticated understanding is missing, then the rejection of Māyāvāda is the rejection of māyā, and the person becomes entrapped in the enjoyment of the falsities of this world—after all, if Māyāvāda is false, then this world is real, whatever exists in this world must also be true. As more and more of this world is accepted as true, the statements like "I love you" are believed to be true just because they exist. So, one must be very careful. The simple-minded rejection of Māyāvāda means that one falls into māyā. And the adoption of Māyāvāda makes one detached from this world but leads to the rejection of transcendental reality. There are dangers in both blind acceptance and rejection of Māyāvāda.

The philosophy of Māyāvāda and māyā is thus not merely for satisfying intellectual curiosities. A good understanding of this philosophy leads to detachment from the material world and the success of spiritual pursuits. The absence of this understanding either means that one keeps wallowing in the false faith in the material world, or rejects the truth of the transcendental world. Both are dangerous.

Why Dreams Feel Just Like Waking

If you lift a ball in your hand while awake, you feel downward pressure. If you ask a physicist why that is the case, then he will say: This pressure is felt because of Newton's gravitational law – GM_1M_2/R^2 – where G is the Gravitational constant, M1 and M2 are the masses of Earth and the ball, respectively, and R is the distance between their centers of mass. Nature somehow calculates all this automatically.

Now imagine you are lifting the same ball in a dream. You will still feel the pressure in your hand, won't you? But is that pressure because of the Gravitational law acting on the ball, hand and a supposed Earth in your dream? Does your mind (or brain) somehow unconsciously remember G, M_1, M_2, and R, then perform the calculation just in time to produce the same effect? Ask that question to the same physicist, and I'm sure there won't be a convincing answer.

There are a few different possibilities, which arise if we consider the physicist's position carefully.

First, you already know the Gravitational law from birth unconsciously, such that the mind automatically performs the calculation and produces the same experience as a dream. But if that were the case, then empiricism is wrong in saying that we know the world by experience, because we would know everything there is to know—right from birth—as even a child who has never been to school has the same experience.

Second, empiricism is right, and we do get information from the world, but that means that we must have memorized the values of G, M_1, M_2, and R, and then the formula GM_1M_2/R^2 and then performed a calculation, although we cannot remember those values off-hand, nor can we recall calculating the formula. Even if that were the case, you should feel that pressure only for the ball that you have previously held in your hands while awake. If your dream was not your waking experience before, then you could not know how you got all those numbers, and how to explain the dreaming experience.

Whichever position you adopt, empiricism becomes false. Either we know everything from birth, such that observation is not required. Or, we cannot see anything new in a dream that we haven't seen during waking, because without that knowledge, we would not know which numbers to compute.

So, let's take some alternative viewpoints. Suppose you say that both dreaming and waking are simply hallucinations created by our minds. In such a case, there is no external reality, and *everything* is being produced by our minds. This includes you inventing the formula GM_1M_2/R^2, followed by individual values of these things, followed by a computation of these numbers to produce an effect. Every new experience you have is now produced by your mind-brain, which means that the mind-brain stores infinite amounts of information, and has an infinite computational capacity to create experience.

The position of Solipsism (that only I exist), or Idealism (that everything is created by my mind), requires the mind being an *infinite* disk and CPU. Clearly, such a postulate is not impossible, but very unlikely, not just because of infinity, but also the issue of why would you store such infinite amounts of information and have an infinite computational capacity, and yet not *know* anything about it? Solipsism and Idealism not only require infinite resources but your total ignorance about the existence of these resources.

So, now let's consider Realism or the idea that there is a reality out there, to which we access. But as we have seen above, this works well only when we consider the waking state, not the dreams.

Of course, there are serious problems even in explaining the waking state. For example, you can say that the real universe is infinite amounts of information storage (which we call "matter") but where is the CPU to compute all the formulae? If nature is run by mathematical laws, then where are these laws computed? Realism requires that some non-material entity must compute the laws.

But how does that non-material reality interact with the material reality? No scientist can answer this question, which is why Eugene Wigner framed a paradox: The Unreasonable Effectiveness of Mathematics in Natural Sciences.

I think you can recognize that this paradox is akin to a *dualism* between matter and mathematics. If you are pedantic, then it is a dualism between numbers stored on a universal disk ("matter") and a CPU (which is non-material). Now if you insist that the computation could also be material, then you are probably not realizing the problem. If there are N particles in the universe, then you have to compute pairwise forces for each particle pair, and there are ${}_nC_2 = N(N-1)/2$ such pairs. For any universe greater than 2 particles, the computer that can compute such pairs would have to be computing a greater number of equations than the particles in the universe. In short, materialism now replaces non-material mathematical computation with another universe—that is much bigger than the present universe!

Now, the present universe is just a disk storing numbers, and the other (non-material universe) is like a gigantic CPU that computes the equations for *this* universe to work correctly. But since you are a materialist, therefore, you must ask: What powers the gigantic CPU (bigger than the present universe), so that it can compute the working of the present universe? Just so that the CPU works correctly in a materialist hypothesis, there must be another CPU to compute its actions, which would require an even bigger CPU. This leads to infinite universes, each bigger than the previous one, for just *one* universe to work correctly. The "disk" universe is the smallest; the CPU universes are successively bigger.

When you realize this problem, then you are better off with dualism rather than materialism. Of course, you still don't know how the non-material stuff interacts with the material stuff. But it is at least not as ridiculous as saying that my existence in this universe requires infinite other beings to exist, just so that they can compute the laws to power my digestion, blood circulation, breathing, and thinking.

To recapitulate, we have thus far rejected Solipsism, Idealism, and Materialism, as being outright ridiculous ideas. We have

Dualism, which seems reasonable, but we have to solve the problem of their interaction.

We can now turn to Vedic philosophy and explain how this interaction problem is solved. And the solution is that the material reality is *generated* from a formulaic reality. You can imagine the existence of a CPU that generates numbers, and those numbers are the visible world. But those numbers were generated by a CPU using a formula, which is a "deeper-level reality". Thus, each level of reality is both a number and a formula. It is a formula because it can generate a new level of reality. And it is a number because it was generated by a previous level of reality. But even that formula is not applied universally; it is applied only to selective things. For example, Newton's formula is applied to masses, but not to charges. So, that formula is also an *idea,* which we call Newton's *gravitational law.*

This leads to the doctrine of the *three modes of nature.* The mode of sattva-guna is like the idea; the mode of rajo-guna is like the formula; the mode of tamo-guna is like a number. Since you can think of all observable things alternately as an idea, a formula, and a number, therefore, everything is a combination of these three viewpoints. The deepest level reality is a pure idea and does nothing unless the mode of rajo-guna propels it into computing to produce a number. And the grossest level reality is even devoid of rajo-guna so that it is a number, but it cannot generate other numbers. This tripartite nature of numbers is discussed at length in the book Gödel's Mistake.

Vedic texts, and Sāñkhya philosophy specifically, identify several levels of this reality; they are called gross matter, sensed properties (called tanmātra), senses, mind, intellect, ego, moral sense, chitta, karma, and guna. The deepest-level reality is called the guna, or the three modes of nature, which then generate successive levels of reality. In the primordial state, there is only sattva-guna, so it is like a pure idea. Then this idea is computed by the appearance of rajo-guna, and successively many such realities are generated. In a sense, a universe springs out of a pure idea—through a formula—via several stages of manifestation, until you get what we normally call the visible material world of things.

Sāñkhya is a conception of reality in which everything is a

number. But it is not just a quantitative number. Rather, each number is also an idea and a formula. So, each number can generate a new number, but that generation depends on the idea and formula encoded by the previous number. Thus, we need to change our thinking about numbers—they are not just quantities. They are also ideas and formulae with generative capacity. Thus, Sāñkhya philosophy states that the body emerges from the senses, the senses emerge from the mind, the mind from the intellect, which comes from the ego, which comes from the moral sense, which comes from the chitta, karma, and guna, and all this arises because there is a soul, which is also an idea, formula, and number, which was generated by the Supreme Soul. This Supreme Soul needs no other idea, formula, or number to generate it. Since the generative capacity in the subtle reality is very apparent, therefore, it is said that the soul and God are different from matter. But when we recognize that even subtle matter is generative, then this stark distinction fades away. Thus, the cascading succession of generative realities comes to an end with a self-generative reality. By the acceptance of this Supreme Soul, Sāñkhya philosophy becomes a *theistic* view of matter.

Now, we can return to our original question: Why do our dreams seem just like waking? And the answer is that they are being generated by the senses and the mind. They are different than the waking experience in one specific sense—the waking world of material things was also generated by some senses and mind, but *we* did not generate that world. The generative principle is still true, but it wasn't our mind and senses. And yet, we can interact with or know things generated by other minds.

But the "laws of nature" remain the same in the two cases, because the senses and the mind—if they generate things—generate them in the same way. They may not generate some reality; in which case we will not see them. But if they do, then the principles of generation are identical in the two cases. Thus, what we see during dreaming is just like what we see during waking. That is because the senses and the mind are generating the reality according to common principles—from *within* themselves.

The generative capacity of the senses and the mind is considered *superior* to the capacity of the senses and the mind where they access a pre-generated reality. Thus, when the senses know the generated world, then they are in tamo-guna; when they generate a reality, then they are in rajo-guna; and when they seek the source from which they were themselves generated, then they are in sattva-guna.

Similarly, the deep sleep state is considered even superior to the dreaming state, because it the source of the generator from which subsequently things were generated by applying a generative principle. A yogi who can remain conscious during the deep sleep of the body can see the generator reality. Those who can observe the dreaming without identifying with it can see the generating process. And those who can remain detached from the gross body can see the generated byproducts as numbers.

The philosophy of generator-generating-generated is not unique to Sāñkhya. Rather, it is the essential idea that pervades all other Vedic ideas; for example, God is the generator, His Śakti or power is the generating, and the soul is the generated. As a result, sometimes, we can say that the soul is the child of Śakti, and then sometimes, the child of God. The philosophy of soul and God is not different from the philosophy of matter; if either of these philosophies is understood, then both are understood.

What is a Person?

Introduction and Overview

In modern societies, a person is defined as something that has rights. Forests, rivers, mountains, oceans, birds, animals, fishes, and insects are not considered persons in modern societies and hence not given rights. Conversely, corporations are given rights, therefore, they are treated as persons. Moreover, the rights of a person are based on a social contract with the government of a nation, which means that the rights can be changed over time.

Since the social contract is between people and their government, therefore, a corporation of one country is governed by the laws of *that* country. The corporation must comply with the laws of other countries while operating in those countries. Some countries have lenient laws, to never prosecute corporations. The idea of personhood is the foundation of all legal doctrines, and changing that idea can also alter all legal doctrines. But when the concept of personhood varies from country to country based on the social contract between the citizens and their government, all countries uphold different ideas of personhood.

How can a fundamental idea such as personhood be determined by the whims of people? Why isn't there a scientific understanding of what it means to be a person? Why should people treat persons any differently than other scientific topics? This article will try to establish a non-sectarian, non-nationalist, and non-contractual understanding of personhood.

Six Aspects of a Person

In Vedic philosophy, a person is primarily defined as *self-awareness*, which creates the notion of "I". Secondarily, this "I" is also defined as five other qualities of intention, emotion, cognition, conation, and relation. The quality of intention becomes "I wish", "I will", "I want", "I need", etc. It is slightly different from the other four qualities because the "I" and wishing are much closer than "I" and emotion, cognition, conation, and relation. That difference manifests in the addition of connectors such as "am" and "have" between "I" and the attribute of "I". For example, we generally say "I wish" rather than "I am wishing" although we say "I am happy" instead of "I happy". I will return to this distinction shortly to discuss why such differences exist and what they entail for our understanding of personhood.

The other four attributes of the person (emotion, cognition, conation, and relation) are relatively straightforward. The emotional qualities expand the self as "I am happy", "I am angry", "I am sad", "I am afraid", "I am jealous", etc. The relational qualities expand the self as "I am a father", "I am an employee", "I am a citizen", "I am a husband", "I am a brother", etc. The cognitive qualities expand the self as "I am tall", "I am white", "I am fat", "I am pretty", etc. Finally, conative qualities expand the self as "I am walking", "I am talking", "I am writing", "I am cooking", etc.

This six-fold definition of a person is used in many ways in Vedic philosophy. Even our cognitive apparatus is sometimes further subdivided into six mutually underdetermined aspects called percepts, concepts, actions, judgments, goals, and morals. In the same way, emotion, relation, and conation are also divided into six distinct aspects.

Sometimes, these six aspects are merged into three aspects—self-awareness, intention, and emotion are collectively called *ānanda*, cognition and conation are collectively called *chit*, and relation is called *sat*. Due to this 3:2:1 pattern, the *ānanda* component of the self is more complex than the *chit* component, which is more complex than the *sat* component. When a person is depersonalized, everything is modeled based on lawful relationships called "force". That universalization of a corner case greatly minimizes the understanding of *sat* which makes it impossible to understand *chit* and *ānanda*. Depersonalization is hopelessly flawed because all reality is personal in Vedic philosophy.

Hierarchy in the Six Aspects

If a person is not acting or becomes incapable of action due to a disability, he doesn't stop being a person. For example, a person who has lost his hands or legs in war hasn't stopped being a person. Likewise, if some or all of our perceptual and mental faculties are disabled, we don't stop being a person. For example, a blind or deaf person is still a person; a dumb person is still a person.

Then, a person who renounces relations to the world doesn't stop being a person. A person may start living outside society, without family, friends, parents, employers, etc. but he is still a person. Then, an emotionally cold person is still a person. He may not feel compassion, love, pride, or other kinds of emotions, and the reduction of the emotions in a person doesn't reduce their personhood. Finally, a person may give up his intentions—wanting, needing, willing, etc.—but it doesn't destroy his personhood. We may say that he has no personality of likes and dislikes (which I will come to shortly), but he is still a person. This is because there is one aspect of personhood—self-awareness—intact.

There is complementarity between the six aspects (covered in my article The Principle of Underdetermination), which results in the underdetermination of the six aspects by the other aspects. For example, every self-aware person doesn't have the same intentions, emotions, cognition, conations, and relations. A relation underdetermines emotions, conations, cognitions, and intentions. This makes the understanding of six aspects slightly harder, but not impossible. We now define a person in a more nuanced manner.

This nuanced definition is *hierarchical*:

- self-awareness is the highest notion of a person,
- their intentions of likes and dislikes are the next definition,
- their emotions are the next definition,
- their cognitions are the next definition,
- their relations are the next definition, and
- their actions are the lowest definition of a person.

In simple words, if you want to know a person, observing their *behavior* is the least good way to know them, because actions are the lowest definition of a person.

In case you might not know, Behaviorism was a prominent school in psychology that reduced a person to their behavior. But a person is *underdetermined* by behavior—not totally determined, and not completely undetermined. Behaviorism is therefore a failed model for understanding a person. However, every other modern psychological model has failed because these psychologists have never been able to incorporate the *hierarchy* and *complementarity* of six aspects into grasping a person's nature.

Once we understand complementarity, then we can say that there are six ways to know the person. Once we understand hierarchy, then we can say that some of these ways are better than others. Quite specifically, we can remove the lower aspects, but that will not make the person impersonal, because these lower aspects were manifest from the higher aspects as *expansions* of the self-aware "I". Like a root grows into a trunk, which then grows into a branch, twig, and leaf, and cutting off the leaf doesn't eliminate the root, similarly, by removing the lower aspects, we don't destroy the person itself.

Degrees of Material Identification

Once we understand this hierarchical definition of a person, then it is very easy to discuss why we use the term "I wish", "I want", "I need", and "I desire" to describe our likes and dislikes: these things are *closest* to "I", although still not self-awareness (identical to "I"). In contrast, we say "I am happy", "I am sad", "I am angry", or "I am jealous" because these are next lower compared to the personality. The "am" in "I am" puts a greater distance between "I" and the quality that we are referring to.

A further distance between "I" and quality is created when we use "I have"—e.g. "I have morals", "I have goals", "I have ideas", "I have a perception", "I have a body", and "I have a car". In essence, as we go down the hierarchy of personhood, we create greater distance from "I". Since the lower five aspects are separate from "I", therefore, we also use "mine" to describe them: my house, my car, my body, my sensations, my thoughts, my judgments, my goals, my morals, my feelings, my relations, etc.

A Brief Segue to the Past

A few years ago, I tried to describe the three aspects of the soul—*sat, chit,* and *ānanda*—as "I am", "I have", and "I want". The problem was that these terms were not used consistently in English. For example, "I have money" is technically equivalent to "I am rich", and "I have a body" can be technically equivalent to "I am the body". This equivalence arises due to people having different levels of *identification* with things other than the "I". The person who identifies with their body and wealth will say "I am the body" and "I am rich". Conversely, the person who doesn't identify with them will say "I have a body" and "I have money". The man who loves his wife will say "I am a husband" and one who doesn't will say "I have a wife". Someone well-versed in such nuances can figure out the deeper reality from the words, as people put different *distances* between "I" and their intentions, emotions, cognitions, conations, and relations. Due to varying distances, "I am", "I have", and "I want" often become equivalent.

I tried to solve the problem using *contractions*: "I have a body" and "the body has tallness" is *contracted* into "I am tall". But this methodology did not produce clarity, because by contraction I meant reducing the distance to an external quality, due to which the thing that is farther from "I" becomes closer to "I", but unless we begin from "I", mere contraction of sentences to produce a shorter one makes little sense.

Thus, the use of "I am", "I have", and "I want" does not produce the clarity I was hoping for, because it might have seemed clear to me, but not to everyone in the same way based on their level of material identification. Hence, I gave up these terms and decided to limit myself to *sat, chit,* and *ānanda*. I also did not have the heart to say to those who felt confused by my terminology: "you are identifying yourself with things that you are not". Hence, I have now rephrased the problem and I would leave it to individuals to decide.

Confusions About Personhood

Ideally, we should have five different words that attach the

"I" to intentions, emotions, cognitions, conations, and relations, and everyone should have the same level of material attachment to use these five different attachments consistently. Both of these are absent. For example, in Śrīmad Bhagavatam 5.5.8, only two terms—ahaṁ (I) and mameti (mine)—are used. This is quite like saying "I wish" vs. "I am happy", "I am tall", "I am working", and "I am married". In a more technically precise language, we would have to use five different connectors to connect "I" to the five other qualities of "I".

Due to the absence of multiple connectors, multiple levels of material identification, and the inconsistent use of "I am" and "I have", personhood is not understood as six different aspects, of which five are *distinct* but *inseparable* from "I". Inseparability is described in Vedic texts as *manifestation*. The five aspects of intention, emotion, cognition, conation, and relation *manifest* from an "I". If they are not manifest or manifest partially, the "I" is not eliminated. However, if they are manifest, they were manifest from an "I", therefore, we cannot say that the person is just those things. Thereby, we get a complex conclusion: The person can be all those things, and yet, those things are not the person.

This is one of the many forms of Bhedābheda in Vedic philosophy: neither identical nor separable. A more detailed understanding of Bhedābheda is that five aspects manifest from an original aspect, these are complementary aspects, and yet, because they manifest successively, they are *hierarchical*. If we don't use this hierarchical and complementary understanding, we don't understand personhood.

Since this understanding is unknown in modern society, therefore, personhood is misunderstood. The modern view of a person, for instance, excludes all these six aspects and designates it as something with *rights*. Then, animals supposedly don't have rights even though they have self-awareness while corporations supposedly have rights although they have no self-awareness. As a result, animals are not persons while corporations are persons. This is an example of how persons become impersonal and the impersonal becomes a person. In the Bhagavad-Gita, Lord Kṛṣṇa calls the inversion of truth into falsity and falsity into truth a symptom of tamo-guna. Since all legal doctrines in a society are based on the idea of personhood, all legalities become immoralities if they don't grasp the nature of personhood.

The Personhood of a Fetus

One of the classic examples of converting a person into impersonal arises in the case of abortions. The advocates of abortions say: The fetus is not moving, doesn't have a developed brain to have cognitions or emotions, we cannot say that it has an agency or intentionality, and therefore, it cannot be a person. They cannot fathom that even if a fetus has no relation, cognition, conation, emotion, or intention, it can still have self-awareness. That self-awareness is the primary definition of "I", not the other things. When the other things manifest, they are manifest out of the "I" progressively and hierarchically.

For example, the fetus will first develop intentions, then emotions, then cognitions, then relations, and finally conations. These are also developed progressively, like a tree develops some leaves, before the twigs, branches, and trunks thicken to produce more trunks, branches, twigs, and leaves. Therefore, even when the fetus moves in the mother's womb, it doesn't mean it has fully developed intentions, emotions, cognitions, conations, and relations. Those things will continue developing slowly even after the child's birth, and in most cases, they keep growing over the course of one's lifetime. Older people, for instance, are more skilled, better at social relationships, and have better emotional intelligence.

The question is: What is the source of all these properties of personhood? And the answer is that they emerge from self-awareness, which is the primary definition of a person. Of course, we cannot perceive that self-awareness, because it might often not have any visible effects. However, because it eventually produces visible effects, therefore, we must accept that there is a person. A cause can be inactive, and we might say that we don't know if it exists. But we cannot say that there is no cause unless we see an effect because, by that definition, something would not be a gun unless it has killed someone. The gun exists as a potential even when it hasn't caused an effect. We can confirm the cause's existence by its effects. However, while that is not confirmed, we cannot deny the existence of the cause. Rather, we have to subject the cause to the appropriate conditions to manifest its properties before we conclude its true nature.

Personhood in Vaishnavism

The six aspects of personhood have numerous manifestations in Vaishnava theology. For example, there is a five-fold manifestation of Nārāyaṇa, Vāsudeva, Saṅkarṣaṇa, Pradyumna, and Aniruddha, from Balarāma. These five personalities constitute the Pāñcharātra system of worshipping God because it is understood that God is one "I", however, there are five successive manifestations from this person. By these manifestations, God is known better, because we see more of His aspects being exhibited.

Similarly, in Gaudīya Vaishnavism, there is a five-fold manifestation of God's persona described as Chaitanya, Nityānanda, Advaita, Gadādhara, and Srivās, which are called Pāñchatattva and are manifest from Kṛṣṇa. Worshipping them together is the worship of the complete form of Godhead, Kṛṣṇa. However, even if we just worship Kṛṣṇa, then we have worshipped the other five since they are manifest from Kṛṣṇa. Thereby, the Pāñchatattva system of worship is philosophically identical to the Pāñcharātra system. The Pāñchatattva system of worship is somewhat superior to the Pāñcharātra system because Kṛṣṇa is the origin of Balarama as well.

There are numerous such five-fold manifestations discussed extensively in various Vedic texts. The book Conceiving the Inconceivable discusses and summarizes many of these five-fold manifestations in the introduction of the book. Personhood is not an easy concept, because it has six aspects. The progressive manifestation of these aspects, followed by their subdivisions, creates literally infinite forms of God. For example, as we noted above, cognition itself can be divided into six aspects of morals, goals, judgments, concepts, percepts, and actions. Since the manifestation occurs progressively, therefore, one form manifests another form. All these forms are based on the same philosophy of personhood. We just have to understand what we mean by a person before we try to understand the *Complete Person*.

Śrīmad Bhagavatam describes 24 incarnations of God and then states in 1.3.28: *ete cāṁśa-kalāḥ puṁsaḥ kṛṣṇas tu bhagavān svayam*, which means "These and the *aṁśa* (parts), *kalā* (parts of *aṁśa*), and *puṁsaḥ* (the parts of *kalā*), are but (the parts of) Kṛṣṇa who is *bhagavān svayam* (the complete form of God). These forms are successively manifest in different ages for different types of pastimes. To understand all of them—which constitutes *theology*—we have to grasp why a person is not simply "I", but five other aspects of that "I", which through successive divisions create infinite variety.

Vaishnava theology thus seems immensely complicated if we try to understand the many forms of God. It becomes much easier if we try to understand *personhood* prior, which is just the understanding of what it means to be a person.

Personalism vs. Monotheism

In Vedic philosophy, there is *nothing other than God*. Even the infinite number of material universes, infinite number of souls, and infinite forms of God are simply varied parts or aspects of a Complete Person. Thereby, there is a relative preference for the worship of the Complete Person over the parts and aspects of that person, but even the universe is personified as Virāta Rūpa (Cosmic Form) of God. Hence, before anyone tries to understand the Complete Person, he or she is urged to understand the Cosmic Form or the Complete Universe.

Similarly, all living entities such as demigods, humans, beasts, birds, fishes, and trees are parts of God. They are entitled to respect in the order of their manifestation from God. Thereby, demigods are superior to men, men are superior to beasts, which are superior to birds, which are superior to fishes, which are superior to plants.

This hierarchy implies that if we have to sacrifice something, it must always be the sacrifice of a lower form of life to preserve the higher form of life. Likewise, if such a sacrifice is performed, it must be the sacrifice of the lowest form of life possible or available in a given situation.

In simple words, if plant food is available, then we have to always begin with plant food. If we cannot get plant food, then we can kill fish. If we cannot get fish, then we can kill birds. If we cannot get birds, then we can kill beasts. There are hierarchies within each of these classes of species too. For example, a cow is the least deserving of death among the beasts. It is better to eat a dog than to eat a cow. Such dog-eaters we considered the lowest of mankind formerly, and are called Śvapaca in the Bhagavad-Gita.

Anything that doesn't follow this strict order is in violation of the natural hierarchy of life-forms manifested from the original life-form, God. Hence, everyone has to kill something to eat. But they have to start at the bottom of the hierarchy and rise up only if the bottommost is unavailable. By such consumption, one part of God is sacrificed to preserve another. But just like you won't cut off your head to save your legs, although the reverse is possible, similarly, the strict hierarchy has to be observed.

Monotheism is a very specific idea—everything other than God is separate from God and hence *not God*. Personalism is also a very specific idea—everything other than God is a *part* of God. This constructs a progressive hierarchy in which there are infinite partial aspects of God (including the material nature), and then there are *atomic parts* like the soul.

The atomism of the soul is that it cannot further divide into parts to manifest other souls. However, since nature can divide into parts, therefore, nature is superior to the soul. Nature, however, cannot love God in the same way as the soul—nature acts only upon God's direction and not voluntarily—however, the soul can also act voluntarily. This voluntary capacity for action is the reason that the soul is called superior to material nature. This is, however, not the only sense of superiority. Nature is superior because it can subdivide but the soul cannot.

Contradictions of Monotheism

Monotheism contradicts Personalism in numerous ways: (a) all species other than humans are not persons, (b) demigods don't exist, (c) nature works according to laws rather than due to persons (see my article Nature Is Governed by Persons Not Laws), (d) nature and souls are separate from God, (e) myriad aspects and parts of God are rejected as polytheism, (f) God loves everybody, but He sends so many to eternal hell, (g) even those who go to

God's kingdom are not loving souls but those with self-serving contracts with God, (g) a worldly person is defined as one with the ability to sign self-serving contracts with another, and (h), over time, even the impersonal entities are legally personalized by giving them the ability for contracts.

In any logical derivation, if your premise is a person, then the conclusion can never be impersonal, because how can you have a logical derivation in which the conclusion contradicts the premise? We don't have to analyze the entire derivation to know that it is wrong. We can know that it is wrong simply from its *structure*, namely, that the conclusion contradicts the premise. This contradiction is introduced very early in monotheistic theology by keeping nature and soul separate from God. Thus, everything derived afterward is false. This falsity has been obscured by the fact that monotheistic doctrines have borrowed ideas from many cultures, some of which were less flawed than others. By mixing things, you can delay the inevitable. Hence, we see the contradictions much later, but if we trace the problem back to where it started, then we will know that the derivation was flawed from the very beginning.

In Vedic philosophy, what is derived from a person, is always a person. We can never produce anything impersonal from a person because that constitutes a logical contradiction. Thereby, everything is a person with different *natures*. That means, they have different intentions, emotions, cognitions, conations, and relations (and some of these may even be absent). Those differences don't mean that they don't have self-awareness. We may not be able to observe their self-awareness, quite like we don't see self-awareness in a fetus and consider it impersonal. That is our ignorance about how myriad variety can be manifested from an "I". If we understand this simple principle, then we will understand why monotheism is not personalism, and we can stop discussing their similarities.

Implications of Personhood

The idea that God is a person, and everything else is manifest as a person from God, changes every single subject.

Personalism changes theology because there are many partial

aspects of God, which can still manifest other parts, and hence they are called the many forms of God (unlike the soul which cannot manifest other souls). Those many forms of God are not many "Gods". They are aspects of a complete person. Likewise, personhood changes all legal doctrines. For instance, animals and trees are now persons, while corporations that don't have self-awareness and cannot manifest intention, emotion, cognition, relation, and conation on their own are not persons.

Similarly, personhood changes the concepts of material science, because nature is not unconscious anymore. Nature might not manifest emotions, but every material object "perceives" certain other objects and acts in relation to them like other persons, based on the contextual relations between things. Nature also has intentionality. Nature cannot be impersonal just because it doesn't express emotions.

In Vedic texts, material nature is personified as Durga, who is called *giri-nandini* or the "daughter of a mountain". She has a stoic, forbearing, and resilient character. You could say that She is almost like a mountain: Rigid, unchangeable, strict, and tough. She is the mother of the material world, and what we see as impersonal and fixed in this world is a reflection of Her *persona*. But it is incorrect to call a stoic, fixed, strict, and tough person a non-person. Personalism is not restricted to feelings and emotions. Therefore, those who worship and meditate on Durga, acquire Her stoic qualities. This worship is better than the weak emotional condition of most people, but not the highest state of perfection because a person who experiences a wide variety of feelings without being weakened is better than the stoic.

Thereby, the worship of Durga is recommended in Vedic texts, to become stoic like Her. The worship of other forms of God is recommended to acquire other qualities. The worship of Kṛṣṇa is recommended for a person to acquire the quality of joy and love.

Kṛṣṇa's joy is not temporary and love is not weak. Unlike material love, the loving nature of Kṛṣṇa has all the qualities of resilience and stoicism. Hence, it is difficult to understand Kṛṣṇa's nature, because He has all the qualities of Durga as well. Kṛṣṇa is the complete form of Godhead because His nature includes all other natures, although they are exhibited to varying extents in different contexts and in relation to different persons who may want to see Kṛṣṇa in more than one way. Thus, Kṛṣṇa becomes a killer of demons sometimes. But that is a rare thing. Most of the time, He is playful, joyful, romantic, and unassuming. His Durga-like nature is displayed rarely.

The fact is that everyone doesn't *want* to acquire the quality of joy and love. Many people just want to be stoic. Due to this variation in their desires and aspirations, the Vedic texts recommend the worship of different partial forms of God, which are parts of the complete form.

People who understand the philosophy of personalism do not argue and fight between themselves. They know which forms of God are superior, and yet, they prefer one form over others. Those who don't know the philosophy of personalism fight to assert their superiority. Then there are people who want to dissolve all forms to eliminate the fights, rather than learn the philosophy of personalism. Both positions are wrong. It is wrong to create contradictions between different forms of God, and it is wrong to merge them all into one.

Personalism, therefore, changes every conceivable subject that we may be interested in. It is the unifying thread that can help us understand everything using the same principles. Every other approach is incomplete or inconsistent, which means that it can never unify our understanding of all the subjects, and either we don't know those subjects, or we think of them in contradictory terms. If we grasp personalism instead, then by understanding one subject, we can understand every subject, because the basic underlying principles of all subjects are the same. Otherwise, learning each subject is like crossing a different kind of ocean, and is impossible for anyone.

The Self as the Basis for Science

Article Introduction and Overview

In several places, I described a semantic conception of reality in which all reality is like a book, comprising symbols of meaning. The book expands out of an idea, and the individuality of the idea divides into the individuality of chapters, paragraphs, sentences, words, and phonemes. Once this expansion has occurred, we can say that the book is the idea, but the idea is not the book. The idea can exist without the book, but the book cannot exist without the idea.

These semantic notions of reality, in which everything is meaning, have seemed too radical to most people. In this article, I will illustrate an even simpler articulation of the difference between modern science and the Vedic description of matter—quite surprisingly—based on a better grasp of the ideas of soul and God in Christianity and how they led to modern science.

The contrast between Christian and Vedic views of the soul is that between the idea of independent individuals and that of simultaneous identity and difference between individuals. If these theological differences of personal identity are grasped, then the differences in the description of the material world resulting from a self-ideology in religion become easy.

This article discusses the differences between the ideas of soul and God as they are found in Vedic philosophy and Christianity and how these two ideas lead to radically different conceptions about matter. The modern scientific conceptions of matter are based on the Christian doctrines of soul and God, and a different scientific conception of matter is possible based on the Vedic doctrine of soul and matter. This article describes those differences.

The Evolution of Vedānta Philosophy

Before we get into the discussion about the differences between the Christian and Vedic conceptions of soul and God, let us spend some time understanding the Vedic conception of soul and God, and how it has evolved in Vedānta.

The most fundamental idea in Vedānta philosophy, beginning with Śri Rāmānuja Āchārya, is that the soul and God are not *one* and not completely *different*. Śri Rāmānuja described the soul as a *property* of an *object*, where God is the object, and the soul is the property. He also distinguished between two kinds of properties, which he called *chit* and *achit*, and identified them as soul and matter. The implication of the object-property relationship was that soul and matter have no *independent* existence apart from God. Rather, they are always tied to God, just like a property of an object is tied to the object.

We have to grasp the novelty of this thesis in the context of the philosophy of Śri Shankara Āchārya, who had made an absolute distinction between Brahman and māyā. He identified the individual soul as a combination of Brahman and māyā and claimed that if Brahman separates from māyā, then the individuality of the soul merges into Brahman because that individuality is caused by māyā. This merger of all individuality into Brahman by the removal of material conditioning is called the doctrine of Advaita Vedānta.

Aside from rejecting the idea of this merger into Brahman, Śri Rāmānuja Āchārya also rejected the separation of matter from Brahman. Most people today may not appreciate this idea enough as they think that God is separate from matter. That separation *is* the philosophy of Śri Shankara Āchārya. However, in the philosophy of Śri Rāmānuja Āchārya, matter is also tied, bound, or attached to Brahman, quite like a property to an object.

The idea of the soul as a property of God leads to some problems. One of these problems is that the material body is also a (temporary) property of the soul and it is a (permanent) property of God. The technical issue is: How can the *achit* property (the body) become the *property* of the *chit* property (the soul)? If instead the body is not a property of the soul, then how can we describe the worldly association between the soul and the body?

For example, if weight and height are two properties of a table, then how can weight become the property of height, such that we would say that this *height* is *heavy*? The impossibility of such a view makes this position seemingly false. Of course, such a problem doesn't arise if we conceive properties in terms of sensations. For example, if color and taste are two properties of an apple, then taste can become the property of color, such that we can say that the color is sweet. Qualitative properties can be attached to other properties, not just to objects. Therefore, the argument of Śri Rāmānuja Āchārya is correct, however, it seems false if we think in terms of physical properties.

To solve this problem, a revision to the relationship between soul and God stated that the soul is actually a *part* of God, not a *property*. And the relation between the soul and the body is the relation between two parts. Just like you can hold your legs by your hands, similarly, the soul can be caught in the body due to a relation between two parts. Even this position, however, leads to some problems. For instance, if a part of my body—e.g., my hands were burnt—then I as the whole person would also be suffering. This would mean that one person's suffering would be the suffering of everyone, including God's suffering. For example, if the material body is burnt, then a part of God has been burnt. Just as burning of the hand causes pain to the person who owns that body, similarly, any material change would change God, and God must therefore be suffering due to these changes. Likewise, the parts of my body—e.g., my hands—cannot act except under the direction of the whole. That would, however, imply that the soul must not have free will.

Then, to solve the problem of God's suffering and the soul's free will, another Vedānta doctrine stated that the soul and God are completely separate. This too leads to some problems. For instance, if soul and God are eternally separate, then how can God be considered the cause of all causes? How can He be the creator and controller of everything? Instead, all individual entities (material and spiritual) must be completely independent of each other.

In this way, the evolution of Vedānta doctrines has been problematic. Either there is no individuality, and therefore soul and God must not exist—then, we can only acknowledge the reality of Brahman and reject the individuality of soul and God. Or, soul and God exist, but there is no conception of soul and God that is consistent with all the things stated in the Vedas, namely:

1. God is the creator and He creates everything from Himself,
2. The soul and the world are in one sense part of God,
3. And yet, if the soul suffers, then God doesn't suffer; if the material body is burnt, then God's body is not burnt,
4. Matter works under the control of God
5. The soul must also work under the direction of God, and
6. This devotion between soul and God is the pinnacle of religion.

Alternative Vedānta Interpretation

All these problems in previous Vedānta interpretations lead to the necessity for a new interpretation, even to explain, understand, and elaborate on the relationship between the soul and God. These are also the issues that the book *Conceiving the Inconceivable* tries to address. It solves the abovesaid problems in the previous interpretations, by which all Vedic statements can be accepted as true, without creating an inherent contradiction.

The essence of the solution, shown in the above book, is a *semantic view* in which soul and matter are part of God, and yet, different from God. This is consistent with the goal of Vedānta beginning with Śri Rāmānuja Āchārya, that soul and God are not *one* and not completely *different*. The Vedānta Sutra speaks of this property as *Bhedābheda* or simultaneous oneness and difference. Since no Vedānta position has thus far been able to explain how this oneness and difference is possible (without contradicting some or other Vedic statement), therefore, a new interpretation of Vedānta is necessary.

We can understand this semantic conception of reality by using two concepts—one abstract and the other contingent. The abstract idea is the whole, and the contingent idea is a part. There are infinite such concepts, but for illustration, we can use two such ordinary concepts. A cow is a mammal, but a mammal is not a cow. A chair is furniture, but furniture is not a chair. This type of identity and difference applies to *universals* or concepts. Then, another kind of identity and difference appears in the case of *individuals*. Again, there is a whole individual and a part individual. For instance, God is a soul but the soul is not God. By pleasing God, I am pleased, but by pleasing myself God is not pleased. This type of identity and difference applies to *individuals*. Finally, the third kind of identity and difference appears in the case of *relationships* due to which we can say that a father is always a man, but a man is not always a father. This identity and difference manifest in the different roles enacted by individuals, such that the same person is sometimes a father, sometimes an employee, sometimes a citizen, sometimes a son, and so on. When he is not exhibiting fatherhood, we cannot say that he is *not* a father. In such cases, the person is a father and yet not a father.

The essence of the semantic understanding is grasping these three kinds of identities and differences. And if these three forms of *Bhedābheda* are understood, then all problems in Vedānta are resolved. Now, we can say that God is the whole, and the soul is the part. But since the soul is also different from God, therefore, when the soul suffers then God doesn't suffer. However, if God is pleased, then the soul is also pleased. Thereby, God is also a soul, and yet, a soul is not God. The soul has to work for God's pleasure, and that is also the soul's pleasure. And this is the highest understanding of religiosity.

The Christian Concept of Soul and God

While the Vedānta system has been trying to explain the identity-and-difference between soul and God, Christianity has relied exclusively on the difference between soul and God. In Christianity, only Jesus as the son of God is "in Christ". Everyone else is separate from God. This creates a problem: Why should Jesus be the only son of God? Why can't everyone else in the world be a son or daughter of God? Similarly, if God is our creator, but we are not the son or daughter of God, then we are effectively disowned children. Christianity asks the disowned child, who is not accepted as the son or daughter of God, to worship God. Why should a disowned child, who God doesn't consider His child, worship the father? There is seemingly a clear paradox between "our Father in heaven" and the idea that Jesus is the only son of God. However, since Christianity insists that only Jesus is "in Christ" hence a distinction between soul and God is created, although there is no distinction between Jesus and Christ. This distinction is at the root of many other problems.

Then, God creates the material world *ex nihilo*—i.e., from *nothing*—rather than from Himself. Therefore, how the material world appears is problematic. One consequence of this problem is that evil exists in the world, but evil could not exist in God. So, what is the origin of evil in the world? Not only by the ex nihilo creation something is created out of nothing, but that something now has properties that did not exist in God. Why would God create an evil world when He was creating the world from nothing, so there was no necessity for the world to have any evil in it. He could have created the world without any evil. Since God created an evil world, therefore, He must be evil.

Thus, by emphasizing the *difference* between God and His creations—soul and matter—rather than an identity-and-difference, deep theological problems are created but Christianity has not been eager to solve them. Christianity rather takes the difference doctrine for granted and advances it. The advancement is that since the soul and God are different from each other, therefore, all the souls are also different from each other. Similarly, because matter and God are different from each other, therefore, different objects in matter are also different from each other. This gives rise to the idea of radical individuality by which the material world is comprised of *independent* particles and various living entities are *independent* of each other. This radical independence now creates everything else in modern thinking. For example, a society is comprised of independent individuals, who must compete with each other for their selfish interests, and the only cooperation between them is through contracts. Likewise, even though material particles are independent of each other, they have a contractual relationship between them established by some "natural laws".

The only difference between soul and matter is that matter follows the laws without understanding them, while the soul understands these laws and then follows them. Since the soul can understand the laws, it can change the laws it creates, and the understanding of natural laws if they are proven false. That ability to change the contractual laws, and the understanding of the natural laws, define the soul's free will (even as the contract binds the soul, the ability to change the contract creates freedom). Since the soul's free will is eternal, therefore, a continuous evolution of social laws and the understanding of laws in science is not spiritually detrimental. Anything not spiritually detrimental is not encumbered by the Church. Thus the possibility to be ignorant and immoral is rationalized as "free will".

Semantic vs. Physical Views of Reality

The physical conception of the material world has thus originated in the idea of a *difference* between God and matter. The soul's power to dominate matter has emerged out of the idea of a *difference* between soul and matter (the soul has free will, but matter has no free will). And the contractual relationship between soul and God has emerged out of the *difference* between God and soul. Through these three kinds of differences, there is so much emphasis given to the difference, that their identity is completely ignored.

In contrast, in Vedic philosophy, the relationship between soul and God is not contractual because the soul is a part of God, and has to serve unquestioningly. God has not disowned His child. Rather, the child has abandoned the father. This child cannot exploit material nature because matter is also a part of God. In fact, matter is the mother through which the father gives the child a material body. So, the soul exploiting matter or trying to dominate the material world is like the child trying to dominate its mother. The soul must have a loving relationship with other souls because these souls are parts of God. Thus, without collapsing the distinction between soul, God, and matter, an *identity* between them is posited, which not only changes religion, but also science, sociology, economics, and politics.

To understand this simultaneous identity-and-difference, a

semantic conception of reality is required in which there are three kinds of *Bhedābheda*—universality, individuality, and contextuality. If we don't accept this semantic conception, then we might be in *difference*—i.e., the Christian conception of matter, soul, and God. However, if we accept the *Bhedābheda* philosophy, which posits simultaneous oneness and difference, then we must change not just religion, but also science, economics, politics, and sociology. Therefore, the semantic conception of reality is necessarily tied to *Bhedābheda*, just as religion or the relation between soul and God are tied to *Bhedābheda*.

Christianity, Advaita, and Bhedābheda

Many Christians are presently frustrated with the radical difference between soul, God, and matter, and they seek solace in Advaita which collapses all these differences. There is always the possibility to go from an extreme conception of difference to an extreme conception of identity. If one makes that transition, then one can say that everyone is "in Christ" although the new term would be "in Brahman". Thereby, everyone would be just like Jesus, and they can be just like God, as Jesus is God in Christianity. That solution to the problems of difference has become very popular at present.

However, with this radical oneness, which lies at the opposite extreme of radical difference, we cannot formulate a science, sociology, economics, and politics. The ideology of radical difference can produce a science because we can at least formulate laws, contracts, properties, and individualities. However, the ideology of radical identity cannot produce all these things because we have no basis on which to explain why there are many things, how they interact, why they interact, and the results of those interactions.

Therefore, there is a third alternative of *Bhedābheda* which is identity-and-difference, and it avoids the problems created by the extremes of either identity or difference. The trouble is that if someone is inclined toward difference, then they are not going to understand the ideology of identity-and-difference. For instance, they will continue to speak about soul and God as two different entities, but they will also continue to think of science, sociology, economics, and politics in the same way as they were thinking of these subjects based on the religious ideology of radical difference and individuality. Conversely, if someone is inclined toward identity, then they will find all these subjects—e.g., science, economics, politics, and sociology—as an utter waste of time, as their goal is the destruction of identity.

Thereby, two extreme reactions to *Bhedābheda* are created. At one end, are those imbued with the idea of radical difference and individuality, and they fail to see why a semantic view is needed; they might say that all this semanticism is false, imaginary, or unsupported by Vedic scriptures, although they cannot explain *Bhedābheda* in any other way. Without explaining *Bhedābheda* they cannot teach the science of the relation between soul and God to intelligent people. Instead, people will either move toward radical individualism, materialism, and atheism, or its opposite—the dissolution of difference, identity, and individuality into impersonalism.

At the other extreme, are those apathetic to a scientific understanding of reality because science is only about matter, matter is separate from God, whereas the soul is nearly identical or identical to God. These people also cannot appreciate *Bhedābheda* and see how the material world is also part of God, created from God, and dissolved into God. Their rejection of *Bhedābheda* can now lead to oneness with God, and while they espouse devotion to God, they remain unaware of the complex characteristics of God. Their impersonalism is translated into a philosophical simplicity that is useless in the real world. They can espouse religion as a subject that is based on pure faith, but that doesn't appeal to an intelligent person. The unintelligent people who take to religion can practice it as a fanatic devotion to God.

Bhedābheda Entails the Semantic View

The principle of *Bhedābheda* is not limited to matter. It applies to everything—soul, God, and matter. In matter, *Bhedābheda* means that the parts are identical and separate from the whole. For instance, you cannot say that an individual is separate from society, and you cannot say that the individual is identical to society.

In terms of material objects, you cannot say that the leg of the chair is separate from the chair, and you cannot say that the leg is identical to the chair. Finally, in religion, we cannot say that the soul is separate from God, and we cannot say that the soul is identical to God. The logic, system of reasoning, conceptual background, and the worldview that we use to understand matter in science therefore also apply to religion.

Therefore, it is not incorrect to say that modern science has emerged from an individualistic and separated idea about the soul and God, which was then extended to matter to produce modern science, sociology, economics, and politics. That is the ideology of radical difference, individuality, self-centrism, and beneficial contracts. While we can collapse individuality and contracts to conceive oneness, that would also not be completely satisfying.

The ideal conclusion must be *Bhedābheda* which requires semantic thinking, which requires radical changes in the understanding of the material world, and that overhaul of science would then reflect within religion too.

The philosophy of devotion is that when the soul suffers then God is not suffering. However, if God is pleased, then the soul is also pleased. How can we have it both ways unless we say that there is an identity between soul and God when it comes to happiness and a difference between soul and God when it comes to suffering? If there is a radical difference between soul and God, then one person's happiness must be independent of the other person's happiness and devotion would be unnecessary. However, if there is a radical identity between soul and God, then the suffering of the soul must also be the suffering of God. Thereby, God must also be poor, fallen, conditioned by the material world, suffering in a material body, and thus no longer God.

Bhedābheda Requires a Semantic Logic

To understand, teach, practice, and perfect the philosophy of devotion, one has to perfect the ideology of *Bhedābheda*. And that means rejecting the extremes of radical difference and radical identity. Since these two logical extremes have to be rejected, the solution seems logically impossible. After all, how can two things be *neither* identical *nor* different? This is a *logical* inconceivability in the sense that *Bhedābheda* is beyond logic, and Śri Chaitanya, therefore, prepended *Bhedābheda* with Achintya.

But what seems beyond logic can be logical, if we change the view of reality upon which this logic is based. The modern concept of logic is founded on the ideology of radical difference. In this logic, two things have identity only if they are the same thing. Thereby, if the soul is not identical to God, then the soul must be completely separate from God. Impersonalism also operates under the same logic and it says: For me to be happy, everyone must be happy, and that is only possible if we collapse the distinction between all individuals because I cannot make anyone happy unless I am them.

Thus the doctrines of both radical separation and radical identity operate under the same logic of either identity or difference. Thereby, a person accustomed to one can move to another with relative ease; at least, a logically inconceivable position of simultaneous identity-and-difference is not involved in the move. In that sense, the ideologies of radical identity and difference have more in common with each other than with *Bhedābheda.* But those who come from a background of separation think that *Bhedābheda* means separation between soul and God. And those with a background of identity think that *Bhedābheda* means the identity of soul and God. Factually, neither position is correct, but because the positions of radical identity and difference conflate *Bhedābheda* with their position, therefore, they fail to see the radical implications of identity-and-difference. Even if *Bhedābheda* is repeatedly demarcated from the other Vedānta positions, most people surmise that all these doctrinal differences pertain to soul and God, and have little to do with the present world. Specifically, the material world cannot be inconceivable; only the love of God is inconceivable. In this way, the philosophy of identity-and-difference is often neglected, misinterpreted, and ignored.

The fact is that identity-and-difference apply to everything, including material objects. And that makes this world as inconceivable as the relationship between the soul and God. The problems of inconceivability have come to the forefront in atomic theory, because it requires a conception of the parts that are not separate from each other, and yet not identical to each other, which is possible only if we postulate the reality of a whole separately from the parts, and then identity-and-difference between the whole and the part.

The new problem is that we need a system of logic that describes reality as meanings, rather than physical entities. Physical entities can either be identical or different; meanings can be simultaneously one and different. This is the genesis of the problem of semanticism in science: We need to use *Bhedābheda* to describe matter, which is inconceivable in physical thinking, and semantic thinking is the only way to make this idea scientific (otherwise, it will remain inconceivable and unscientific). The Vedic scriptures restrict themselves to *Bhedābheda* as they are not conditioned by the modern conceptions of identity and difference. Both the ideology of radical difference and radical identity are relatively recent inventions. Once we are conditioned by this type of thinking, then identity-and-difference seems illogical. For a mind conditioned to such logic, a change in logic is essential.

Why Bhedābheda is Difficult

However, this change is not trivial, because even the most learned people hold logic and arithmetic sacred. Understanding *Bhedābheda* means rejecting both ideas. For example, because 5 follows 1, therefore, 5 is produced from 1 and whatever is produced from 1 is included inside 1. Thereby, 5 is included inside 1. You might think that 1 is smaller than 5, so how can 5 be inside 1? And the answer is that the bigger number is a smaller meaning because numerous individual entities we count by numbers are parts of the whole that comes first. This also means that you can add any number to 1, and the result would still be 1 because 1 already contains all numbers. Adding other numbers to 1 is like a student repeating the information received from a teacher back to the teacher; that is not going to make the teacher more knowledgeable.

Quantity addition depends on the idea that all individuals are equal. For example, if we add 5 things, then we assume that the things being added are *equally individual* and hence the result is 5. One thing is not a partial individual and the other thing is not a fuller individual. They are all equally individual. But this idea is false. God is a big individual and we are small individuals. Thereby, all individuals are not equal, and if we add five things, and one of those things is God, then the result is only 1 thing. Arithmetic, therefore, depends on the assumption that all individuals are equal. If instead, we understand that all individuals are not equal, then quantitative addition fails. The equality of individuality is a principle we get from religion, and that principle then propagates into the study of the material world.

If instead individuality is qualitative, then some individual is also a superior quality which makes them a bigger person. If we strip the qualities from the person, then each individual becomes equal. Thereby, quantitative addition is the consequence of stripping persons of their qualitative individuality.

I'm making all these points to illustrate how revolutionary the identity-and-difference way of thinking is that it requires us to discard conventional logic and arithmetic. All these rejections are based on the ideas of the self.

The illustration of this fact in religion is that if you add all the tables, chairs, stars, planets, houses, animals, humans, etc. in zillions of universes, then the result would be one thing–God. God is not huge in size. He looks just like we look. And yet, everything is a *fraction* of God. So long as we are conditioned to arithmetic addition as the idea of whole and part, we can never understand how God can be a gurgling baby in an affectionate mother's arms, and yet a physically bigger mother would be a part of His baby-like person. Then what to speak of millions of universes being a part of God. All these things are possible only if we can give up mundane ideas of logic and arithmetic-driven notions of bigness. At the least, the Sāñkhya and *Bhedābheda* philosophies are inconceivable because are we conditioned to logic and arithmetic.

To understand all these things, we have to move over from quantities to qualities. Semanticism means thinking in terms of qualities. God is the original quality. And if we add up all the qualities in all the universes and their components then the result would be one quality–God. In terms of qualities, all these universes embody the partial qualities of God, and so they are parts of God. That has nothing to do with "size". Rather, "size" simply means infinite minor quality variations within a narrow subset of qualities. The greater the granular differences within the narrow subset of qualities, the "bigger" is the universe. Therefore, a huge universe can be created from one pore of hair on God's body. That universe elaborates the details which are summarized and are innately present within one pore of hair on God's body. Since the universe can be compressed inside the pore of a hair on God's body, therefore, all quantitative thinking along with the logic of separated things must be thrown away. That logic of separate things, which then leads to the idea of arithmetic addition is a hindrance in understanding qualitative addition.

The point is simple. Any intelligent person is likely to ask: How can God be a baby in a mother's arms? Isn't the mother bigger than the baby, so the mother is likely to produce the baby rather than the baby to produce the mother? Isn't the mother temporally prior to the child? How can a universe be created from the pores of God's body? How can God appear in this world looking like a human, and yet be the origin of everything? How can the source of everything be inside the thing produced from the source? I would not be exaggerating if I said that there are millions of such questions. Thousands of years are required to even compile all these questions. But all of these questions have one answer: Think in terms of qualities, use the *Bhedābheda* system of reasoning, and you can answer all the questions yourself.

The Simplicity of Vedānta Philosophy

Factually, *Bhedābheda*, semantic thinking, and Vedānta are identical to each other. *Bhedābheda* requires a change in logic, which is the foundation of whole-part thinking, and semantic thinking makes whole-part thinking viable because it helps us overcome its logical contradictions. Thereby, Vedānta means the conclusion of all knowledge, *Bhedābheda* is that thesis within the Vedānta system which reconciles all seemingly contradictory Vedic statements, and semantic thinking is that thesis by which *Bhedābheda* can be understood without creating logical paradoxes. The difficulties we have with semantic thinking are difficulties in visualizing *Bhedābheda* philosophy.

Vedānta, as the summary of knowledge, can be stated as follows: *Think of everything in terms of whole-part logic.* God is the biggest whole, and hence whole-part thinking applies to God and soul. However, chairs and tables are also smaller wholes with parts. Therefore, the whole-part philosophy also applies to chairs and tables. Thereby, the principles of Vedānta apply to God, the soul, and the material world. If we can only understand whole-part thinking, then we have known everything that is to be known.

At present, we reduce the whole to parts, or dissolve the parts in the whole, or subtract a part to reduce the whole, or add the parts to increase the whole. But what we need is the whole that divides into parts, the parts separate from the whole, and yet that the whole is not reduced. These parts are neither entirely separate from the whole, nor are they fully identical to the whole.

Such is the conception of the self in Vedic philosophy. With this sophisticated understanding of the self, we can change the understanding of everything else, because the whole-part way of thinking applies to everything, not just to the relation between the soul and God. Modern science is developed on a separated existence of the soul in Christianity. And a Vedic science can follow the principle of integrated existence of the soul as part of God. The simple difference between separated and integrated soul is responsible for all subsequent ideological differences. Just as a separated thinking of the soul evolved into modern science, likewise, an integrated thinking can evolve into a different science. That science, because it uses the system of whole-part thinking, is perfectly applicable to everything, including religion.

Mistakes in Consciousness-Based Science

Many people like to say that modern science is based on the rejection of consciousness when the truth is that modern science is based on consciousness, although that consciousness has been contaminated by the idea of separated individualism in Christianity. Once that contamination enters the consciousness, then over time, consciousness claims that the consciousness doesn't exist. This is because when one pursues radical individualism, then material nature destroys our freedom. Material nature is designed to disprove our radical individualism by depriving us of control over our lives and thereby the ideas of choice and freedom. When we lose freedom then it seems that we are helpless, and have no choice. Without choice, there can be no soul and without soul, there is no need for God. Thereby, the simple sequence produced from radical individualism is: (a) loss of freedom, (b) rejection of choice, (c) rejection of soul, and (d) rejection of God. When we reach the stage of atheism, then we can keep talking about consciousness, but it doesn't matter because we cannot perceive the existence of choice and freedom. Now, consciousness is also understood as a material phenomenon. If instead, we do see some choice, then the contamination in consciousness pushes us to exploit the opportunities in the world for individualistic ends.

Therefore, it is false to say that modern science is not based on consciousness, and hence we need a role for consciousness in science. The fact is that modern science is also based on consciousness, but those notions came out of the contaminated ideas of the soul in Christianity, and that contamination is destroying the ideas of soul, God, and religion over time. The need, therefore, is not consciousness but *pure* consciousness.

In the Śrīmad Bhagavatam, it is stated that God divides Himself by Himself to create the contaminated consciousness of the soul. God is the whole, and the undivided contamination is His Sakti. God unites with this undivided contamination, which is called the sexual intercourse of Shiva and Shakti, which then produces parts of the contamination as the children of Shiva and Shakti. The soul chooses one such child contamination produced by Shiva and Shakti as its personal identity, and the Sakti then chokes and stifles this identity, which the soul considers its own strangulation. It is like looking at a drama, identifying with a character, then seeing the character being choked, and feeling helpless to conclude that we have no choice. This strangulation of the contaminated identity is as much a byproduct of the contamination as the original idea of independence. The contamination is evolving from one state to another, and the soul is being continuously dragged in the process.

God creates atheism so that we can play with fire and be burned by it. God is not just evil, but He is the greatest type of evil there is. And yet, He uses evil to cure us of evil. You need a scalpel to remove the pus in a wound. The pus is evil and the scalpel is evil, and God creates both. However, we initially enjoy the pus, and later suffer the scalpel. If we did not accept the pus, then there would be no need for the scalpel. Therefore, the material world is fully evil in one sense (except when God and His pure devotees appear in this world to cure the evil), and in another, some evil is the cure for another evil.

Pure Consciousness and Perfect Science

Therefore, it is not enough to talk about the role of consciousness in science. It is more important to talk about the correct idea of consciousness because by that correct idea we can understand simultaneous oneness and difference, and then everything else in analogy to the self. Therefore, atheistic and spiritual sciences are equally based on consciousness. They are only founded on different types of consciousness with different self-ideologies.

Ultimately, the self is always the basis of any worldly manifestation of an idea or thing, and since there are so many worlds, therefore, they are also based on different ideas of the self. The correct diagnosis of modern science is that it begins in a contaminated consciousness and then manifests infinite byproducts. By that analysis, we can say that pure science can also begin in pure consciousness, and then manifest infinite byproducts.

Therefore, before we can change science, we must articulate a different understanding of the self. By changing the conception of the self, which is based on true and eternal love and devotion, a new science can manifest naturally. The mechanism of producing the world from consciousness is already there. We just have to change the consciousness from which the present science was created in order to produce another science.

All our creations are portraits of ourselves, and we create such portraits to know ourselves. The world is a mirror, and it can reflect anything. But what it reflects is who we are. The science that we see today is the proverbial man in the mirror produced as the reflection of a man outside the mirror. The man in the mirror will change if the man outside the mirror changes. Likewise, to change science, we need to alter the self-ideology that created science.

The Soul is Moving and the Body is Not Moving

The first important thing we learn from Bhagavad-Gita 2.13 is that "just as the soul passes from childhood, to youth, to old age, in the same way, the soul passes to a new body at the time of death". Most people take this to mean that after death there will be another life, which is true. But that is not all that this Bhagavad-Gita verse says. It employs two terms—*yatha* and *tatha*. Yatha means "just as" and tatha means "in the same way". So, the transmigration of the soul is not just between lifetimes, it is also within a lifetime. The correct understanding of the verse is "just as the soul is transmigrating from one body to another *in this life*, similarly, there is transmigration *after death*".

Soul Motion vs. Body Motion

The bodies are discrete states and the soul is the continuity between those states. Each body is like a point in space, and the soul is like a particle that moves to construct a trajectory that connects these points. The laws of motion, therefore, apply to the soul, although we would call this the change of body rather than the motion of the body. The body is not an object. It is rather a state of the object called the soul. Childhood, youth, and old age are such *states* of the soul. Modern science is based on the idea of body movement and everything in the Vedic system is based on the motion of the soul from one body to another.

This difference influences all other areas of movement. For instance, the sun globe is not moving in the sky. Rather, the sun-soul is moving from one sun-body to another. The trajectory of soul motion involves meanings (qualities) and the trajectory of an object of motion involves physical points (quantities). The sun-soul moves through qualitative states around the year (which is a day for the sun-soul in Vedic cosmology) like our bodies cycle through the morning (refreshed), afternoon (hungry), evening (relaxed), and nightly (tired) states. By drawing such quality trajectories, we understand how the soul moves from one body to another. The study of sun-soul, and its interaction with other planetary souls, therefore is considered "scientific knowledge" although it is not opposed to "religious belief".

The material universe is now a *space* in which each location denotes a bodily state. This space can expand or contract. When it expands, more bodily states become accessible; for example, new species or new subdivisions within a species become visible. When it contracts, then fewer bodily states are accessible; for example, previous species or subdivisions within those species disappear.

That expansion or contraction of space is the *motion* of matter. Hence, material dynamics is described in terms of five kinds of changes called creation, destruction, maintenance, revelation, and hiding. *No motion*! Why? Because the dynamics of the material energy constitute the expansion and contraction of space, making some parts of the space accessible or inaccessible to the soul, and maintaining that space in a certain contracted, expanded, accessible, or inaccessible state, for a certain duration of time.

The Philosophy of Buddhism

Unlike in Vedic philosophy, where a soul (as a particle) moves to construct a trajectory, in Buddhism, there is no particle although there is a trajectory. That trajectory constitutes transmigration without a soul. This is called *anātma-vāda* soulless consciousness. So, when a Buddhist talks about consciousness, he means that there is a trajectory that connects discrete points. Now, if we remove all the points in space, and just leave trajectories, then there will be no sense of the *passing of time*. You can imagine flying in space that has no planets, galaxies, light, or anything else. It is just an empty space. You can be going a million miles a second, but you will feel no wind on your face, no change in scenery, and no sense of time. Time, according to the Buddhist, arises because there are things that we seem to pass by.

Similarly, the Buddhist will say that if we enter empty space, then we can stop all experience and hence the passing of time. That timeless state is *nirvāna*. To go to that empty space, we have to practice detachment. By withdrawing consciousness from the world, we get a trajectory disconnected from all points. We remove the points from the trajectory, then the continuity is already there.

One of the peculiarities of Indian languages is that negations like *anātma* mean *non-self,* rather than *no-self.* A trajectory is an individual thing, so it is not "no self". We have to say that it is *non-self,* which means that there is no moving particle. A Buddhist does not have a mind-body interaction problem, because the bodies are discrete points, and the mind is the continuous trajectory that connects these points. Moreover, the trajectory can exist without points. It is a continuous thing already. It just appears to be passing through discrete states because we are attached to worldly experiences. If we practice detachment, then discreteness disappears and eternity returns.

The Philosophy of Impersonalism

In this broader context of Buddhist thinking, impersonalism appeared in India to say that there isn't even a trajectory; there is just space, which is called Brahman. From this space, emerge individual trajectories. Yes, there may be no sense of passing time for a trajectory in empty space, but so is the case when a person enters deep sleep. The absence of passing time is not the absence of individuality. To completely destroy that sense of individuality, we have to say that even timeless trajectories emerge out of Brahman. That will destroy the sense of individuality that seems to exist in the timeless deep sleep, although it is not experienced as passing time. This obsession with the destruction of individuality makes impersonalism a place further down the same road as Buddhism. In Vedic philosophy, Brahman is therefore considered beyond the deep sleep state. It is a sense of timelessness without there being a sense of I and mine.

The debate between Buddhism and Advaita was not about whether material objects are moving because it is agreed that they are not moving. It also wasn't about whether the soul is moving because both voidism and impersonalism agree that there is no soul. Their debate was about whether there are an infinite number of timeless individual trajectories or one *space* that temporarily produces these *trajectories.*

The Position in Vaishnavism

Whatever impersonalism called Brahman was redefined as a form of God in Vaishnavism. The creation emerges out of God, like speech from a speaker, and it comprises the souls and material states. Material states expand and contract, and become accessible or inaccessible, constituting the dynamics of matter. The soul moves over these material states constructing its trajectories. The Bhagavad-Gita describes matter and soul as Kṣetra (material field) and Kṣetrajña (the knower of the field). The Kṣetrajña *moves over the* Kṣetra to know it.

Just as we can walk in a park, similarly, the soul is moving over the park called the material field. The park is not moving, rather, the soul is moving. But by that movement, new things are perceived at every moment. The bodies are the Kṣetra in which the soul is walking.

This walk can involve big or small changes. The change at the time of death is big and the changes during life are smaller. But they are always discrete. Unlike impersonalism and Buddhism, where soul and God are unreal, and even experiences are also unreal in some sense, in Vaishnavism, the world is real as a combination of Kṣetra and Kṣetrajña. However, it is not Realist in the modern scientific sense that the body moves in space. Matter is real and eternal, but matter is *not* moving. Rather, the soul is real and it moves from state to state.

Confirmation by Yoga Practice

The practice of yoga is designed to bring this philosophy into experiential confirmation. This is achieved by stopping the movement of consciousness to stop the changes occurring in the mind and the body. For example, in the aśtānga-yoga system, the practitioner first stills the body via āsana. The Pātāñjali Yoga Sutra describes a single āsana called the sukha-āsana or quite simply "a comfortable posture" to still the body. The body is considered stilled if it is perfectly relaxed, and we stop feeling pains and aches. Then, a yogi stills his breath through prāṇayāma. Then they still their senses, which is called pratyāhāra. Then they still their mind, which is called dhārana. Then they concentrate their consciousness on one thing which is called dhyāna. When that consciousness is perfectly stilled, then, it is called samādhi.

Through the progressive steps of stilling that culminate in the fixing of consciousness, the yogi stops aging because aging is the soul moving from child body to youth body to old body. He enters a trance that can last thousands of years. The Kṣetrajña stops walking in the Kṣetra and the Kṣetra was never moving. This is akin to a person standing in one part of a park and watching it. A fixed consciousness leads to a fixed body. The body will start changing again if the Kṣetrajña started moving in the Kṣetra. Until then, there will be no bodily changes.

Even temporary conscious states like hunger, thirst, lust, sleep, etc. involve the movement of consciousness. If we stop the movement of consciousness, then we will not feel hungry, thirst, sleepy, or lusty. Lust is not coming to us; we are going to lust. Hunger and thirst are not coming to us; we are going to hunger and thirst. Sleep and tiredness are not coming to us; we are going to them. Thus, if someone doesn't believe that the soul is moving from one body to another, then they are given the practice to conquer their hunger, thirst, sex, and sleep. As they conquer all these feelings, they realize: The soul is moving from one body to another. However, the body is not moving.

Confirmation by Mantra Chanting

The bhakti-yoga system inverts this process by focusing the consciousness on the sound of a mantra. If the consciousness is focused, then the emotions are stilled. By the stilling of emotions, the thoughts are stilled. Then the senses are stilled, and finally, the body is stilled.

This is a matter of realization by practice, by which we reach the same conclusion: The body is moving *because* the senses are uncontrolled; the senses are uncontrolled because the mind is disturbed; the mind is disturbed due to the ebb and flow of emotions; this ebb and flow of emotions occur because consciousness is not focused. However, by concentrating the consciousness, everything else is stilled.

The body is not moving. Instead, the soul is moving from one body to another. If the soul is stilled, then the body change stops. By stopping the soul's motion, we stop bodily motion. This is explained through philosophy, but it can also be confirmed by sincere practice.

The "Movement" of Material Objects

Even when we see the sun moving in the sky, the soul is moving from one body to another. The zodiac signs like Capricorn and Sagittarius are like the bodily states of the sun-soul. The sun-soul changes these states. The observed movement of the sun is not the movement of a body. It is the movement of the sun-soul from one body to another. If we think of this movement as the motion of a body, then we cannot explain the qualitative differences between the months of a year, the times of day, etc. The time of birth would not matter. These are naturally implied in modern physics, but they are rejected in Vedic cosmology. The reason is that the sun-soul changes his body.

This idea of body movement is entrenched in modern "primary education". As children grow up, they try to solve every problem in terms of some body movement. If the mind is changing from one thought to another, then it must be molecular movement. If our emotions are changing from happy to sad, then it must be some electrons moving. If we perceive a world, it must be due to photon movement.

But there are hundreds of types of changes—the evolution of ideas, the rise and fall of societies, the changes in political ideologies, the shift in cultures, the evolution of language, the changes in fashion styles, the rise and fall of the economy, and so on. In such cases involving collective movement, we cannot even find a moving object. For example, when the economy rises and falls, what is actually going up and down? Can we find an object called the "economy" that is going up and down? Likewise, when some fashion styles cyclically go in and out of fashion, can we find an object called "fashion" that is going around in circles? If we cannot find such objects, then we cannot construct laws of motion. We cannot draw their trajectories. Even if we construct heuristic laws, they will be anti-realist because there is no identifiable object called "economy" or "fashion" and everything does not move in the same way with the "economy" and "fashion" changes.

This is when we have to say that "economy" and "fashion" are not *objects* but *states*. The soul moves through these states. The economy is rising or falling not due to laws about money and value, but due to laws about the soul movement. The evolution of ideas, societies, and cultures is also about the movement of the soul. And this would be consistent with identifiable objects such as our body or the body we call the sun. Therefore, we can extend the idea of soul-movement to every possible kind of evolution. But we cannot extend object movement in this way because we cannot identify a moving object. This is why object motion is a bad idea and soul motion is a good idea.

Matter Is Not Insentient

Material Inertness in Religions

It is well-known that the material energy is personified in Vedic texts as Durga. And yet, starting with Advaita, the Vedānta doctrines have designated matter as *achit*—inert, inanimate, or insentient. Descartes, of course, designated matter as being distinct from the mind in his famous mind-body dualism. Christian theologians have also treated matter as dead and inert.

Since both science and religion agree that matter is inert, therefore, religions do not challenge the scientific ideas of mathematical laws and determinism. Intelligent Design Theories, for instance, accept the laws of modern science as being designed by a higher intelligence (although that higher intelligence may not be called God). Thus, all the disagreements between religion and science appear to be focused on the nature of the soul and God: In modern science, whether they exist, and in other religions, on their real nature.

Thereby, numerous problems about the interaction between the sentient and the insentient are created. For instance, if God is sentient, then how does He control matter? Is He pushing matter like a man pushes a cart? Likewise, if the soul controls matter, then is its will like the gravitational force? In this article, I will discuss the reasons why matter is also sentient, and without such sentience, it is impossible to account for dharma and karma in nature. I will then also discuss the difference between the sentience of matter and soul, due to which they are described as inferior and superior sentience, respectively, rather than sentient and inert.

Material Inertness in Science

In Newton's physics, the inertness of matter is called *inertia*—i.e., its inability to change its state of rest or motion on its own. A force external to an object pulls inertia to move it. Due to the capacity to exert a force, there is causality in matter. So, in what way can we call it inert? The answer could be that matter is moving due to *external* rather than *internal* causality. Internal causality can be spontaneous, like human free will. But external causation requires push or pull. Even this force cannot be due to internal causation—i.e., some free will—to remain consistent with the previous idea that matter has no internal causation. Hence, the external force must be deterministic.

This is where a distinction between the modern idea of matter being inert and the religious idea of the soul being sentient (able to control matter) appears. Since many things—e.g., digestion and immunity—happen on their own, therefore, we cannot say that the soul controls everything. And yet, the soul must be able to control something in the body for it to be sentient. Since religions are unable to explain how the soul can intervene in matter, therefore, scientists will say: We have no free will. There may be an illusion of free will, and how that illusion is created may be unknown. But there cannot be a conscious intervention in the laws of nature, as all laws will then be false.

How the Soul Interacts with Matter

To solve this problem, we have to understand how the soul interacts with matter. The process is complex, but I have recently found a simple analogy to illustrate it. Imagine that you open the YouTube app on your phone. If you are a newcomer to YouTube, the app will show you a wide assortment of videos and try to glean your interests. Your choice is simple: *scroll* or *pause*. If you pause, then YouTube learns your preferences and uses them to show you more videos of the same type that you have seen before.

In the same way, material energy generates desire, impressions, and impulses automatically like YouTube shows you videos. However, you have the choice to scroll or pause. If you keep scrolling, then the material energy will show you something different. But if you pause, it will learn what you are doing—which is called *habit formation*—and show you the same things again and again.

The material energy is addictive in the same way that social media is, and it controls the soul in the same way that YouTube algorithms control the viewer. And yet, by changing your pause-scroll behaviors, you can change the videos that YouTube shows you. Similarly, by associating and dissociating with different phenomena, the soul can change its experiences.

Soul-Matter Interaction Creates History

YouTube must "know" that you have paused the screen. In the same way, the material energy must *know* that you have accepted or rejected some material qualities produced automatically. If material energy is totally insentient, then how can it know what you are doing? Then, how can it tailor your successive experiences? Material energy has to know your choices to create a repository of your "history" and use it to show you successive things. And yet, it can *seem* insentient just like a YouTube app seems to be insentient to all of us.

The "knowing" by the material energy exists as the "history" of our choices. This is like YouTube stores the history of our pauses and scrolls. Spiritual emancipation is the process of deleting this history and exiting the YouTube app. Further progress in spiritual life means using another app in which our history is also stored but those are not the choices of selfish gratification.

The difference between modern science and the science that explains the causality in matter based on the soul's choices is *history*. In modern science, the past doesn't exist in the present, and it has no causal influence on the present. To solve the soul-body problem, we can say that the successive bodies are like successive videos on the YouTube screen, and pausing and scrolling of this succession creates a new sequence of videos. Scrolling means that some thought emerges in our consciousness, and we withdraw our consciousness from that thought; that thought disappears while a new one appears. Pausing means that when this new thought appears, we focus on it, and the thought then develops through successive stages as described in Sāñkhya leading eventually to sensual activities. And the sequence of videos we see is based on the past history of things we have chosen or rejected.

Three Types of Knowledge

You might now counterargue: The history of events or memory of the past doesn't require sentience because even a computer disk can store that history! That is true, but it is not the whole truth, because computer disks cannot store first-person feelings. For example, suppose YouTube shows you videos that you don't like, but you have no other entertainment, so might go on watching some video. YouTube will interpret your selection as a liking, when in fact, you are looking for something better but not able to find it.

Sentience is not required when we are measuring the effects of choices but it is required when we are trying to understand how a person *feels*—happy or sad, excited or bored, angry or calm. By knowing these feelings, we get a true understanding of a person's nature. If we only know a person's actions, we never know the person. Their actions can in fact be interpreted differently based on the interpreter's attitudes toward the same thing. For instance, a jealous person often criticizes others, and he might therefore think that every criticism of others must be based on jealously rather than truth.

This problem also exists in the interpretation of meanings—i.e., *what* a person is doing—but it is most pronounced in understanding *why* a person is doing something. If the observation of actions is complete, then we perfectly know *how* a person is doing something. That doesn't fully determine *what* and *why*. For example, if the sequence of words is *how*, then by reading those words, we cannot fully determine the sentence's meaning—the *what*—because the meaning is also determined by the context in which things are said. Then, even if we know the context, we cannot determine *why* the person is saying so, because that reasoning is the unique individuality of the speaker. Thereby, actions are third-person knowledge, contexts are second-person knowledge, and moods are first-person knowledge. Sentience is not needed for third-person knowledge. It is needed more for second-person knowledge, and it is absolutely necessary for first-person knowledge. The combination of these three types of knowledge is necessary to understand every action completely—e.g., how was something said, what was said, and why it was said.

Why History Needs Sentience

The material energy is sentient because the memory or history of events is combined with their feelings. Hence, we can talk about "happy memories" and "painful memories". However, we can never perfectly understand these feelings without sentience. If matter is not sentient, then there would be events, without meaning and feeling. But we know that the reverse is true.

For instance, we might often forget the exact words spoken by a person (the *how*), but we remember *what* they said. Then, we paraphrase that meaning using our words, expressing the same meaning. Likewise, we might forget even what was said, but we might still remember how we felt about it.

Our memories are structured from why to what to how. How is further elaborated into who, where, and when. As we get old, we forget the times, places, and the persons quickly. Then slowly we forget the exact words, and what was said. We forget the feelings associated with that interaction last.

A computer disk stores the where, when, who, and how. Of course, in Vedic philosophy, even where, when, who, and how are qualities. For example, where is a type of location (home vs. office) not just an address. Similarly, time is good or bad, right or wrong, not just the number on a clock. A computer cannot give where, when, who, and how qualitative meanings, but it can register numbers. A computer disk cannot register the meaning (what) and feeling (why). And without these nuances, it can never equal the memory that we hold. The type of memory we hold requires sentience. And since that memory is stored in matter, therefore, matter has to be sentient.

This sentience explains why so many things work automatically without our conscious intervention—e.g., our automated fight or flight responses, digestion, blood circulation, etc.—although they are conditioned by the past which means that they don't work the same way in everyone. Similarly, the sentience explains why conscious intervention can alter or arrest the automatic activity. Thereby, we can say that nature works automatically for the most part, and yet, it can be controlled by our will. That sentient control of nature is possible only because nature is also sentient and not insentient.

Dharma and Karma in Nature

An understanding of feelings—e.g., what we enjoy and suffer—is essential to karma. If we don't account for a person's feelings, then there is no measure for 'good' and 'bad'. If we don't account for the context, then there is no definition of 'right' and 'wrong'. Then, there would be no way to decide the punishment of the wrong deeds and rewarding of the right deeds. Sentience in nature, however, can reward us according to what we find pleasing, and punish us in the way we find displeasing. Thus, the law of karma, or tit-for-tat, doesn't mean the inversion of the previous actions. It rather means reward and punishment for actions in the way that we will enjoy or suffer.

If we enjoy eating sweet food items and suffer eating spicy food items, but another person enjoys spicy food items and suffers sweet food items, then good karma can be accumulated by feeding the other person spicy food and enjoyed by obtaining sweet food. Tit-for-tat is not the opposite reaction to action in Newton's mechanics (if you push a table by a force F, then the table exerts F back). Action and reaction are rather mediated by a contextual right and wrong duty to decide if a duty was fulfilled or violated, followed by the reward or punishment based on the individual definition of good and bad.

Hence, even the law of karma requires sentience in the form of contextuality and individuality. When such sentience is acknowledged in nature, then we can grasp that even the semantic conceptions of where, when, who, and how are necessary while their physical counterparts are causally irrelevant.

Superior and Inferior Energies

Now, you can ask: If material nature is also sentient, then why is it called the "inferior energy" while the soul is called the "superior energy"? The answer is that the material energy cannot love the Lord in the same way that the soul can. The material energy is like a servant of the Lord—the Lord asks for something, and the material energy fulfills it. However, the material energy will not do anything *voluntarily* for the Lord—i.e., without His asking. The soul can, however, do things for the Lord even if He doesn't ask for them. Due to its voluntary nature, the soul can do things that are *contrary* to the Lord's will, or things compatible with the Lord's will, although not requested by Him.

We can illustrate this difference through the following simple example. In a restaurant, the chef makes the items that we ask for. The chef, however, will not make those items unless we ask for them. In contrast, a mother will cook for her child those things that they will enjoy even though the child hasn't asked for them. The material energy is similar to the chef who will cook only those things that are ordered by the Lord. And the soul is like the mother who will happily cook items for the Lord's pleasure even without being asked.

Both the chef and the mother are sentient beings, but the mother exhibits the qualities of love whereas the chef does not. The chef can in fact know far more recipes and have greater expertise in cooking compared to the mother. But the mother's cooking is more satisfying because it is done with love. When you order something in a restaurant, there is no element of surprise. But if a mother cooks for her child, then there is an element of surprise. When the surprises are always pleasant, then the happiness is greater. That happiness makes us say that the mother's cooking is better than restaurant food.

In the same way, material energy is far more accomplished, powerful, and capable than the soul. However, the soul is still superior to matter because of its capacity to love the Lord in a way that material energy cannot. Hence, there is no contradiction between Durga being the controller of material universes, and the soul being a small puppet in the material world, and yet, the soul still being called the superior energy relative to matter. The soul's superiority is based on love, while Durga's superiority is based on power and capability.

Insentient Ideas of Matter

Starting with Advaita, many in the Vedic tradition have equated this superior and inferior distinction to sentient and insentient, completely disregarding the fact that material energy is also a person. This idea is also accepted in Christianity, leading to the claim that the soul is empowered to exploit material nature. After all, matter is insentient, so no one is being hurt in the process. This idea then crept into modern science through Cartesian mind-body dualism, where matter is insentient, while the mind is sentient, thereby creating a schism between religion and science as dealing with two separate domains (science with the body and religion with the mind). As the study of matter based on insentience progresses, it rejects the existence of the soul and God which were previously considered sentient because it is impossible to explain the interaction between the sentient and the insentient.

The problem is that when religions counter atheism, they are half-guilty of advocating that matter is insentient. Many people thereby talk about consciousness not being a product of dead matter. However, they cannot explain how the sentient intervenes in the working of the insentient. If the insentient matter is working according to mathematical laws, then God and the soul are not in control. Then, why do we need the soul and God, if they are not in control of the material reality? Why, in fact, would we need dharma, karma, and reincarnation, if there is no volitional control over matter?

To solve that problem, we have to begin with the idea that matter is not insentient. In fact, matter has the same properties of sat, chit, and ānanda as the soul. Hence, there is a capacity to know the soul's activities, meanings, and feelings quite like a sentient being knows another. The sentient being called matter may not love the soul, and it is hard for the soul to love such a sentient being, but the absence of love doesn't mean that the other person is not sentient. After all, don't we interact with thousands of sentient beings who do not love us, but who are truthful, righteous, and well-intentioned?

Religion Must Reject Insentience

We cannot completely fault modern science for atheism because religious theories have had the same adversarial view about matter, which led to mind-body dualism and then to the rejection of the mind. If instead matter is also sentient, then the soul-body interaction is an interaction between two souls.

That interaction can be modeled as a conversation between two persons. Whatever we call "inert matter" is like words exchanged in a conversation. However, behind those words there is a mind with meanings. Behind those meanings are three kinds of judgments involving the truth, good, and right (which involve the intellect, ego, and moral sense). Those three judgments employ three kinds of criteria, namely, universality, individuality, and contextuality. And behind these three criteria is the will of the souls that *choose* the assumptions or axioms about what is true, right, and good.

Now, it is very easy to study matter: Matter is like a moderated discussion forum, in which souls converse. Each soul starts with some assumptions and considers them true, right, and good. When they speak, a historical record of their conversations is created, which moves them from one conversation to another, one forum to another, in the process modifying their assumptions of what is true, right, and good. The creator and moderator of the discussion forum moves the participants until they arrive at the perfect truth, right, and good. Then, the soul moves into another forum and conversation—the spiritual energy—where the truth, right, and good don't change. The charge of insentience is easily dropped when all the conversations are intelligent, appropriate, and pleasing. However, the charge of insentience is false even when the conversations are unintelligent, inappropriate, or displeasing.

The Vedic religion describes matter as a personality called Durga. She is like the chef who can cook anything for us, provided we can pay for it. But just because She will not cook unless we can pay, doesn't mean She is insentient. When things seem to work automatically, it is because we are not needed in Her kitchen. When we suffer, it is because She has restricted the choices for us on the menu. The automatic working of nature, the restriction of choices, and the working based on our demands are all based on sentience in nature.

Advaita falsely claimed that Brahman is sentient and māyā is insentient. This idea was then carried forward in other Vedānta doctrines like Viśiṣṭādvaita and Dvaita. This idea also exists in other religions and modern science. Hence, most people accept it unquestioningly. Then, they are embroiled in intractable problems such as mind-body dualism, the rejection of soul and God due to the partial successes of insentient modeling of matter, and the conflict between religion and science. Then, some people say that matter is intelligently designed, because they are trying to solve the science-religion conflict, without solving the mind-body dualism or how the sentient can control the insentient. Factually, there is no solution to any of these problems except that which begins by accepting that matter is also sentient.

Consciousness Expands by Concentration

The physical dogma about the world is that as you look deeper inside things, you get to know smaller and smaller parts of the world. As a result, by looking deeper, you lose the big picture. Thereby, there is a contradiction between depth and breadth. You can be a jack of all trades and a master of none. Or, you can be master of one trade, and know nothing about anything else.

Withdrawing the Consciousness

This physical dogma is easily refuted experientially by those who seriously meditate. Meditation means the concentration of consciousness. The Bhagavad-Gita states: The yogi withdraws his consciousness like a tortoise its limbs inwards. When the consciousness is withdrawn, then the senses are withdrawn, the mind is withdrawn, the intellect is withdrawn. By these withdrawals, superficially, we stop knowing the world. But paradoxically, by this withdrawal, we know more about the world than by looking at it.

When the consciousness is withdrawn, concentrated, and focused, it begins expanding such that the greater the concentration, the greater the knowledge of reality. Thereby, the contradiction between depth and breadth is dissolved: Going deeper within is knowing the broader reality beyond the self.

The Philosophy Underlying Meditation

The reason for this paradoxical outcome is the transcendent and immanent nature of truth. The concept of mammals is transcendent to cows, dogs, horses, and tigers. And yet, the concept of mammal is immanent in cows, dogs, horses, and tigers. So, if you want to know the meaning of mammal, you can potentially study all the cows, dogs, horses, and tigers (and all other types of mammalian species) and if you have completed the study of all possible species then you can claim to know the mammal. But you can also look within a single species and try to fully understand that species to know a mammal.

In the former case, you are going 'outward'—i.e., studying all the species. And in the latter case, you are going 'inward'—i.e., studying just one instance of one species. The latter is how we understand humanity; we don't have to know every human to know what human means. We know the meaning of a human by knowing ourselves, although we are just one of the many humans.

Physical Ideas Hinder Knowledge

And yet, the physical dogma has conditioned everyone to believe that mammals and humans are never *in* anything. These are simply words used to describe collections of things. At best, humans or mammals may represent DNA, but you cannot know that by knowing yourself. Rather, you have to look through a microscope to understand the DNA to define a human or a mammal.

If, however, you look into the microscope, what you see is not what you experience yourself to be. Thus, a contradiction between first-person and third-person knowledge is created. And this general pattern continues endlessly—even the knowledge obtained through different third-person methods produces contradictory pictures. For example, the picture of society and economy contradicts the picture of reality in physics, biology, cosmology, psychology, and so on. Nobody knows how to reconcile these pictures.

Transcendence and Immanence

The problem of unity and diversity is resolved in Vedic philosophy by stating that there is only *one* reality—God—but He has infinite *aspects*. The whole truth—God—is within each aspect, such that the whole truth can be known from each aspect, and yet, the whole truth transcends each aspect.

This is the paradoxical transcendent and immanent nature of God. If God were not immanent in each thing, then it would be impossible to know Him except by knowing everything, which would be impossible for any finite being. But if God was confined to one of these things, then He would be at most those things and not God. This problem is solved by a *trinity* called Brahman, Paramātma, and Bhagavan. Bhagavan is transcendent, Brahman is all His aspects, and Paramātma is immanent in each of the aspects.

The soul or the self is one of these aspects, and it is part of Brahman. However, the whole truth is immanent in the soul, therefore, by knowing itself, it can know the whole truth. We don't have to endeavor to know the entire reality in order to know the entire reality. We just have to know ourselves completely, and by that process, we will know the entire reality. This is the philosophical foundation of meditation—withdraw the consciousness inward and as it finds that which is immanent in the self, it will also find the whole truth, which is transcendent and includes everything beyond the self.

This principle applies to matter as well. As the consciousness withdraws from the body to senses to the mind, intellect, ego, and so forth, it climbs up an inverted tree from leaf to twig to branch to trunk to root. This rising consciousness naturally reveals the nature of the subtle material reality, of which the gross reality is a part, quite like the concept yellow is part of the concept color, and the concept color is part of the concept seeing. So, withdrawing consciousness is the process of knowing the reality even more.

Theory and Practice of Meditation

Concentrating the consciousness is the method for *expanding* consciousness. Expansion means that we know more and more. And we know more and more by withdrawing from trying to know it. This idea is inconceivable in physical thinking and it can only be realized through meditational practice.

It can also be understood theoretically if we give up physical thinking and embrace semantic thinking in which the whole truth is inside every partial truth, the partial truths are within the whole truth, and yet, the whole truth is transcendent to the partial truths. However, if we continue under physical thinking, then the emphasis on the withdrawal of consciousness seems to entail that the goal of life is not to know reality, that the external world is an illusion, or that any attempt at knowledge is a waste of time.

The fact is that the goal of meditation is knowing everything, and withdrawing from knowing individual things is the process of knowing everything. So, there is no contradiction between a yogi who abandons the world to meditate vs. the attempt to know reality via philosophy. The yogi hasn't abandoned the pursuit of knowledge; he is rather pursuing the method of concentration to expand consciousness. Similarly, one who has expanded the consciousness to see the presence of God in everything need not abandon the world, because that detachment is for one who hasn't yet expanded the consciousness. Meditation and knowledge are methods to the same goal.

Then, even those who have not seen God in everything can use the world like wealth is used to serve the owner because, by that process of finding the best way to serve God through the things in the world, they will begin to see which things are more like God's nature, and which things are dissimilar to His nature. That is also a process by which to understand God's nature. Thereby, prvṛitti (engagement with the world) and nivṛtti (detachment from the world) are both considered feasible methods for realizing the same complete truth.

The engagement with the world, however, is an inferior method to knowing the truth because there is much scope for misunderstanding, misconception, and misdirection. The concentration of consciousness is a relatively better process for expanding consciousness because the pitfalls are fewer.

Methods to Improve Meditation

The issue is that most people cannot concentrate their consciousness. Therefore, a compromise is reached—(a) try to philosophize as best as possible so that you have more conviction about meditation, (b) try to detach yourself from the world progressively so that your senses and mind are less distracted about the occurrences in the world and you can meditate better, (c) while you are not detached, try to see the presence of God in everything such that if your mind is preoccupied with thinking about the perfect truth, as the meditation will then be easier, and (d) try to perform all your moral duties.

The fact is that most people cannot follow this compromise because (a) there is little capacity for philosophy, (b) there is strong addiction to sensory stimulation, (c) there is no intuitive ability to see God in the world, and (d) there is very little skill to distinguish between the real and imagined duties.

Therefore, even this compromise is further reduced to one injunction: Serve the self-realized soul. Just do whatever he says. Don't worry about what he means, why he said this, and the outcomes of following his instructions. Just do it. This is the point at which most people revolt. They abhor the idea of being someone's unquestioning servant. They like their independence.

Knowledge is fine because it is independent. Detachment is fine because it is independent. The vision of God in everything is fine, as it is independent. Doing our duties is fine because it is independent. But becoming someone servant? That is not fine. People forget that we arrived at this solution after two levels of compromise—(a) we could not concentrate the consciousness, and (b) we could not follow the four-pronged process of knowledge, detachment, duty, and mysticism prescribed as a compromise.

Now, if we cannot follow the solution of concentrating the consciousness, and then we cannot follow the four-pronged compromise solution given above, and then we cannot follow the compromise to the compromise (i.e., surrender to the advanced soul), then there is probably no way for us.

The Path of Obedience and Surrender

If we obey (which is a very big if, because nobody wants to give up their false pride), then we get everything else gradually, including the ability to concentrate the consciousness. Then, the soul also becomes independent, and yet, he never becomes disobedient. He always considers himself the menial servant, ready to do whatever is asked for. Obedience means to do what has been asked for by the spiritually advanced soul, not second-guess, analyze, or speculate on what it really means, and why it was asked. When we obey, then we get the realization of what it really means. But if we cannot give up our independent mentality and want to *understand* before we *obey*, then there is very little hope, because we will never understand, and we will never have the capacity to do anything independently on our own.

In this way, a self-reliant process of meditation becomes dependent on obedience to a spiritually advanced soul through a succession of steps: (a) we cannot concentrate our consciousness, (b) we don't have the intellect to understand philosophy, (c) we are unable to become detached from the world, (d) we don't have the perceptiveness to see God in this world, and (e) we are unable to decide what is morally dutiful in a given situation. The irony is that the process of complete surrender is also rejected by almost everyone due to false pride because now people equate this as a path reliant on faith rather than reason, individual endeavor, and the perfection of the self.

Religion is not about faith. It is about the concentration of consciousness to perceive the complete truth. When that truth is perceived, then knowledge, detachment, duty, and vision of God in everything are attained automatically. Then, there is automatic respect for other spiritually advanced souls because that respect and faith are based on prior direct experience and realization.

However, religion becomes dependent on faith because of our own inabilities. Then if we reject the process of faith out of false pride, or out of the need for independence, then all doors to true knowledge are closed prematurely.

If we cannot do anything else, at least we can be honest about our true capabilities. Honesty devoid of false pride can lead us to surrender not because it is the only path, but it may be the only path for us.

The advanced soul doesn't want mindless slaves. He wants sentient, intelligent, enthusiastic, loving, and creative individuals. However, this independent thoughtfulness results from a process of concentrating the consciousness and using knowledge, detachment, moral dutifulness, and vision of God in this world, to overcome the shortfalls in any such practice. If even the methods that improve the concentration of consciousness are lacking (e.g., the intellect is not sharp enough for philosophy, or the mind is attached to worldly enjoyment, or that one cannot distinguish between real and imaginary duties, or one lacks the perceptiveness to see when the innate qualities of God are present in this world), then it is better to become a mindless slave to an advanced soul, than to be thoughtlessly independent.

How Do You Know You Are Not Dreaming?

The Role of Dreaming in Philosophy

Vedic teachings talk about the four tiers of reality, called waking, dreaming, deep sleep, and transcendent. Each successive stage of reality is given greater importance, which means that dreaming is more important than waking. This surprises people—We dream when we sleep; how can sleeping be more important than waking? In this article, I will discuss why dreaming is more important than waking, and by that inversion, the waking world is modeled in Vedic texts after the dreaming instead of modeling the dreaming after the waking world.

For example, if dreaming is a reality in the mind, then even wakeful reality that is often indistinguishable from dreams must be like the mind. That is, even the waking reality should comprise sensations and ideas rather than "material stuff"; the space in which we see the world must be like a mind, and the events succeeding each other must be just like the evolution of a dream from one percept and concept to another. It doesn't mean that the external world doesn't exist. It just means that it is modeled in the same way as a dream.

After making these distinctions, we will then discuss how we distinguish dreams from waking. The simple idea is that my identity is immanent in my dreams, and similarly, the object's identity is immanent in the waking perception. By checking that immanent identity, we can know if my perception is a dream or a waking experience. Without that immanent identity, we cannot distinguish between waking and dreaming. Since most people are able to distinguish waking from dreaming, the problem is the physicalist conception of reality that rejects immanent truths and makes it impossible to understand how such distinctions are made. To understand how we distinguish dreams from waking, we have to model the external world like our senses and mind—the sense and mind are the "space" and percepts and concepts are "objects" in them. The objects appear out of space and disappear into space.

The Mechanism That Generates Dreams

Logic is broken now because the mind is the thought but thought is not the mind. If we insist on preserving logic, then we get the quantum problem in which the six questions of why, when, where, how, and who has which dream is unanswerable, leaving us with probabilities. The mind is now like a dice—every moment we toss it to get a different percept and we have hit a dead end.

To solve that problem, the probabilities must pertain to the unconscious from which conscious experience springs. The unconscious is the space and the conscious is the object springing out of space and collapsing into space. The unconscious is many hidden thoughts, but the conscious is one thought at a time. They are distinct as conscious and unconscious and they are identical as the mind. Thereby, the mind is the thought (dreaming) and thought is not the mind (unconscious). We cannot use classical logic because one thing is two things—but if we use it, then we get incompleteness in which we can only talk about the probabilistic unconscious and not about the factual dream.

The paradox is that the conscious can be unconscious—its opposite. When the same thing is two opposite things, then the Principle of Identity collapses and leads us to a logical contradiction. The resolution of that contradiction is that the conscious becomes unconscious and the unconscious becomes conscious. One thing transforms into its opposite, so it is both, neither, and each.

We explain these things by hiding and revelation. The unconscious is hidden when the conscious is revealed, and vice versa. Thereby, the opposites hide each other, reveal each other, exist inside each other, exist outside each other, and are sustained by each other. Everything is like that, including opposites like hot and cold, bitter and sweet, big and small, heavy and light. Thereby, logic fails for everything. As I have discussed in my writings (see article The Implications of Compression and Incompressibility), binary logic is a false approximation of an inseparable reality into binary separable things.

Extroverted and Introverted Approaches

There is a deep-seated assumption in the modern view of perception, which is called the bahirmukhī or "extroverted" idea of experience—the cause of my experience is something other than me. For instance, a physicist might say that a photon emitted from an object hits my eyes and becomes my experience during waking. However, with this model of photon emission and absorption, we cannot explain dreams because the eyes are closed during dreams.

We can explain dreams only if the experience springs inside out—from the unconscious to the conscious. In fact, even while waking, images still arise automatically, which are no different than the images you perceive with your eyes closed. The antarmukhī or "introverted" person examines these experiences and concludes: If these images are arising inside-out with eyes closed, or even with them open, then all experience must arise inside-out.

The introverted person then progresses from the dreaming stage into the deep sleep stage, also known as the unconscious. In Sāñkhya, the unconscious or the deep sleep is described as one's guna, karma, and chitta. That unconscious becomes a dream and to be consistent, the same approach must be followed for a waking experience. The difference between dreaming and waking is that there is no external correlate of our experience during dreaming, but such a correlate exists during the waking experience. Correlation, however, is not causation.

Correlation and Causation

For instance, if I am slapped, then the true cause is internal—guna, karma, and chitta—and this cause creates an opportunity to be filled by someone outside me. That opportunity is a "hole", that sucks someone with the ability and desire to slap me. If that "hole" was not created, then the opportunity will not exist, and I will not be slapped. Hence, slapping is the combination of opportunity, desire, and ability. The person who slaps me has the ability and desire, but my guna, karma, and chitta create the opportunity. The inner cause pushes me to a place, time, and role where I become the opportunity for someone to use their ability and fulfill their desire for slapping. If one person isn't attracted to the hole of opportunity, then another will, until the hole of opportunity is filled by sucking someone into it. My slapping ends only when the hole is destroyed.

Thus, from my perspective, the chitta, guna, and karma are *necessary* and *sufficient* to determine my getting slapped—necessary because I will not get slapped without it and sufficient because even if one person doesn't slap, someone else will. When a cause is necessary and sufficient then it is complete. The person who slaps me is incidental to my being slapped. While such a person exists during waking, he doesn't while dreaming; a self-created image can also slap me. The extroverted person sees a correlate and attributes slapping to him. The introverted person sees the cause to be within himself.

The Emphasis on Introversion

The extroverted person says: If I lock myself into a room, then I will not be slapped. The introverted person says: I can be slapped in a dream, and there is no experiential difference between getting slapped during waking or dreaming. The extroverted person's outside-in model of causation will attribute causation to something other than himself. But if the same person becomes introverted, then he will analyze their dreaming experiences and say—waking and dreaming are two ways of explaining the same experience. Hence, they should be explained in the same way. Even when I'm awake the cause of my experience—e.g., perceptions, thoughts, judgments, and emotions—must lie within me.

This attitude toward self-analysis becomes prominent through meditation too, when we try to control our minds and prevent the automatic emergence of perceptions, thoughts, judgments, and emotions. We realize that our minds are not in our control.

So, what causes the emergence of my experiences? That question takes a person to the understanding of the unconscious, namely, chitta, guna, and karma. We cannot perceive these but we can perceive their effects. Hence, the theory of the unconscious has to be accepted on *faith* although it is not *blind faith*. Faith is required because we cannot see chitta, guna, and karma. But blind faith is not required because we can perceive their effects. A similar kind of faith is involved even in physics—e.g., you cannot see the gravitational field but you can see its effects. A cause accepted on faith is justified when it can explain *all* possible effects—i.e. when it is complete.

The Rejection of Extroversion

Dreams are good examples of testing such faiths. For example, if you lift a heavy object in your dream, you experience a downward pull. You cannot explain this downward pull based on gravity because gravity necessitates a force exerted by something other than you, and its effects are observable to others. But a dream is confined to you and the results of you lifting weights in a dream will not be observable to others. The introverted person asks: If I must explain the downward pull during a dream without gravity, then why should I rely on gravity to explain the downward pull during waking? The extroverted person instead disregards the dream of lifting weights as being irrelevant to science.

The introverted person rejects gravity and says: The experience of downward pull is a property of the object-concept in my mind, rather than of the external object. When that object-concept appears in my mind, it acts on the sense of touch to produce the effect of a downward pull, even if there is no external correlate. Therefore, we must attach the property of "weight" to the object-concept, and explain it through a hierarchy of ideas—the object-concept, the property of weight, and a value of that property as lightness or heaviness. Similarly, we must say that the object-concept is in the mind, but its appearance in the mind has an effect on my sense of touch to create the percept of heaviness. Since the object-concept can appear and disappear, therefore, mass and energy are not conserved. An entire world can appear and disappear in the dream, and it is not conserved. But there has to be an explanation for this appearance and disappearance without invoking conservation.

Explaining Both Truth and Falsity

That's when we talk about unmanifest and manifest. The unconscious reality is that which is unmanifest, and dreaming or waking experiences are their manifestations. The unmanifest can be converted into the manifest by self-action during dreaming. It must also be manifest in a similar same way during waking, which means that my chitta, guna, and karma produce an image of the world, even when there is an external correlate. Thereby, the external correlate can be a snake but my image of it is a rope. That misperception is caused by my chitta, guna, and karma, and it doesn't exactly correspond to reality.

Similarly, when I correctly picture the external rope as a rope, the internal picture is still caused by my chitta, guna, and karma. Therefore, true and false perceptions are *my* product, not reality. That doesn't mean the external reality doesn't exist. It means that I am causally necessary and sufficient for my experience since I can see a rope as a snake or as a rope, or I can see a snake or a rope in a dream. Three out of four—(a) rope as a snake, (b) rope in a dream, (c) snake in a dream—are false, while one out of the four—rope as a rope—is true. The falsity is much bigger than the truth, even if we just use two concepts—i.e., rope and snake. As the number of concepts grows, the total number of falsities grows exponentially and overwhelms the truth, because the truth is now very small. The theory of experience must explain both falsity and truth.

Modern science relies on extroversion and Sāñkhya on introversion. Both are empirical and rational. But the empiricism of Sāñkhya gives greater importance to dreams while the empiricism of modern science disregards dreams and tries to marginalize the scope of waking experiences to instrument measurements. Even if you speak about sense perceptions to ordinary people, they will always attribute their causation to others rather than themselves. Then they will come up with theories involving mass and gravity, conservation of energy and mass, and so on. All these scientific theories are easily invalidated for the introverted person because he asks a simple question—When I lift an object in my dream, I feel heaviness, although there is no external world. When a world is not necessary for my dreaming experience, then instead of making theories about the world, I should be making theories of experience. Those theories include the experience of the world, so they are more *complete* than the theories that explain the world but preclude my dreams. More complete is also *truer*.

Truth-Falsity Rational Distinction

Now we can ask: What is the difference between lifting weights while dreaming vs. while waking? I will consider two possible answers to this question—one that is more extroverted and the other that is more introverted one by one.

The extroverted answer is that nobody else experiences my dream, and hence, when I lift weights in my dream, there is no change to anyone else's experience. This extroverted answer is better than talking about changes to the world, because of the age-old question: "If nobody saw a peacock dance in the forest, then did the peacock really dance?" The answer to that question is: The peacock could have danced in his dream, and in that case, we could say that he danced but nobody knew about it. But if the peacock danced in the forest while waking, then the trees in the forest would have an experience. The peacock's dancing would be a correlate of the tree's experiences, while their cause is internal to the tree. The problem is that the tree has no way of knowing that its experience is correlated to a real peacock's dance. The tree's experience could also be a dream, instead of a waking experience. This extroverted answer fails because we don't know when someone else has an experience, even if we see them, because that process of seeing someone seeing me, could just be my dream.

The introverted answer is that additional karma is not created during dreaming, but it is created during waking. For example, immoral actions during dreaming don't deserve punishment, and moral actions during dreaming don't deserve rewards. Guna and chitta are still modified during dreaming—e.g., thought experiments are often used to determine possible courses of action and how we might prepare to avoid or bring about such situations. By such contemplation, we develop desires (change to guna) and abilities (how to handle the situation or bring about the desired outcome). But you can contemplate a nuclear war, and such contemplation will not invite rewards or punishments.

The introverted answer is that a part of the unconscious—i.e., karma—is not created during dreaming but is created while waking. If I explode a nuclear bomb in my dream, I'm not a criminal to be punished. If I do charity in my dream, I'm not a saint to be applauded. However, by dreaming about such things I may develop a proclivity (guna) and ability (chitta) toward violence or charity. That increased proclivity and ability may then lead to violent or charitable action which is why contemplating such things may be good or bad. But as long as they are still dreams, they are not to be rewarded or punished.

Hence, if we rely on an extroverted approach to determine if we are dreaming or waking, we can never find the answer because every dream can be reality and every reality can be a dream. The difference can only be known if we try to construct a causal explanation of our experience, and the difference is that good actions during dreams do not lead to rewards while waking, and bad actions during dreams do not lead to punishments while waking. This incongruity between the succession of experiences cannot be explained without designating some experiences as dreams and waking. Since that incongruity can exist, hence, we can say that dreams and waking can be distinguished *theoretically*.

Incorrect Truth-Falsity Empirical Distinction

This may not satisfy many people, because the theoretical claim is complex. They might ask: Can we not rely on the experience itself to decide if we are waking or dreaming? There are a couple of incorrect answers to this question.

First, we call something waking experience if it matches our *memory* from the past. For example, if I walk from one room to another, I have the memory of seeing furniture arranged in a certain way. My memory creates the *expectation* of seeing precisely those things. To the extent that the expectation is fulfilled, my present experience matches my memory from the past, and I might conclude that I'm awake. If the expectation doesn't fully match the present experience—e.g., if the furniture has been rearranged—I still consider myself awake although to reconcile the memory with the present, I say: The furniture was moved by someone. I don't have the memory of moving the furniture myself, so I attribute the movement to someone else. Of course, those suffering from memory loss also think that someone else is doing things when they may have done them themselves although they don't remember doing them.

Likewise, if you go to a new place that is not part of your conscious memory, but there are unconscious impressions of such a place from the past, you may think that I have been here before, although you cannot tell the precise time when you have been there. The problem is that we can match our present experience to our memory even during dreaming. For example, people having traumatic dreams match their present experience with past memory and think that it is real. Therefore, we cannot rely on memory to decide if I am awake or dreaming because (a) memory is unreliable, and (b) we also rely on memory during dreaming and believe that it is waking rather than dreaming.

Second, we can call something waking experience if it follows some standard rules of behavior. For example, water boils upon heating, the room becomes cool upon turning on an air conditioner, etc. Many dreams are so outrageous that we don't expect such things to happen while waking. For example, I can have the dream of flying in the air by flapping my hands, but such a thing won't happen while waking. Therefore, I could claim that we distinguish dreams from waking because dreams do not follow the same laws consistently. But even this distinction depends on my memory of the laws of nature.

If I don't have a memory of how the world behaves, or I suffer from amnesia of the laws, then I will not be able to distinguish waking from dreaming. Similarly, if have unconscious memories of a different type of lawful behavior, then the match between memory and experience would make me think that these bizarre experiences are actually my waking experience. Again, we cannot rely on memory to decide if I am awake or dreaming because

(a) memory is unreliable, and (b) we also rely on memory during dreaming and believe that it is waking rather than dreaming if we have bizarre memories.

Correct Truth-Falsity Empirical Distinction

The correct answer to this problem involves the use of Satkāryavāda from Sāñkhya and Arthavāda from Mīmāṃsā. Satkāryavāda says that the effect is present within the cause. Arthavāda says that the cause is present within the effect. We can also call these two doctrines the transcendence and immanence of cause and effect. Under Satkāryavāda, the effect is immanent in the cause but the cause is transcendent to the effect. Under Arthavāda, the cause is immanent in the effect, and the effect is transcendent to the cause. Hence, we can know the cause from the effect, and the effect from the cause. By knowing the effect immanent in the cause, we can say that the cause is sufficient to produce the effect. By knowing the cause immanent in the effect, we can say that a cause necessarily produced this effect. If either of these two conditions is dropped, then we lose the necessity and sufficiency of causation to get indeterminism.

The effect is just like an email that carries the sender's and receiver's addresses on it. The receiver is obviously the person having the experience, but the sender can be the observer or some other. During a self-created dream, the dream is like an email in which the sender's address is the self. During a waking experience, the experience is similar to an email in which the sender's address is something other than the self. Dreaming is therefore like a person sending an email to themselves while waking is like a person sending an email to someone else. You can look at the two emails, and check the sender's address on them. If the sender's address equals you, then it is a dream. Otherwise, it is waking.

Immanence and Unmanifest

The senses and the mind have the capacity to generate percepts and concepts and process percepts and concepts. That processing includes reading the sender's address, which is *immanent* in the percept and concept. By reading this sender's address, the senses and the mind *can know* if the percept or concept is self-generated or received from someone else. The sender's address in the email, however, exists as an immanent truth that cannot be separated from the letter or email body. We can separate the email body from its headers (which include the sender's and receiver's addresses) but we cannot do so with the immanent reality. It is as if every word in the email has the sender's address imprinted on it. The immanent presence of the sender is also sometimes described as the "speaker in the speech". An author is immanent in the book, a musician in their music, a poet in their poetry, and an artist in their art. By seeing that immanent reality, we can know the author, musician, poet, or artist from their creations, and by knowing the creator we understand the creation.

Materialism disregards this immanent presence because you cannot see the immanent truth by cutting it up. Factually, if you tear a book into pieces, you will not find the author, because the author is still immanent in all the words. Even after tearing a book, you can read one of the pages, and say: These are the words of a specific author. This immanent presence is described in Bhagavad-Gita as avyakta-mūrtinā or an "unmanifest form" that becomes manifest to the perceptive mind or the senses but remains hidden or avyakta to others.

There is hence a mechanism by which the mind and the sense know that "this is not my creation" or that "this is coming from somewhere else" because they don't see themselves reflected in the concept or percept. But if the mind and the senses have been dulled such that we can only see the "surface" reality and not the "deep" reality, then we will only see percepts and concepts and not their source in them. Then we cannot distinguish dreams from waking.

Similarly, if we don't understand that the source is immanent in the percept and concept, then we can keep arguing endlessly about the inability to distinguish between dreams and reality because we are only looking at the "surface" and are incapable of seeing the "deep". When the senses and the mind are dulled, then the philosophical problem of distinguishing between dreams and reality arises because the person with the dulled senses and the mind also remains ignorant about the immanence of the cause in the effect, and cannot distinguish between the self-created dreams and the externally-triggered reality.

Applications of Immanent Truth

A similar problem arises in distinguishing the self-created mental noise from the thoughts inspired by the Paramātma in the heart. If we can read the sender's address in the thought, then we can know which thoughts are self-created and which ones are inspired by Paramātma. Even to be guided by the Paramātma, we need to distinguish between the self-created mental noise and Paramātma's inspiration. Without it, we would always be controlled by the mind rather than letting Paramātma control it, and divine inspiration loses meaning.

Another example of this issue is the "brain in a vat"—a thought experiment in which a brain is kept in a vat, connected through wires to a computer, into which an evil programmer has installed malicious software to control the brain by injecting electrical impulses into it. The argument mimics the Cartesian "evil demon" controlling the mind. Descartes escaped this problem by claiming that God's benevolence precludes the existence of such a demon. The materialist, however, removes God from the argument, postulates an evil demon controlling our minds, and asks: Can we know whether we are controlled by an evil demon who is simulating all our experiences? Their answer is: We don't. It just proves that by removing God from the Cartesian argument, we lose realism.

The real answer is that the source of experience is immanent in the experience and a perceptive sense and mind can know the source from the experience and thereby determine that this experience is caused by the evil demon. However, this requires us to perceive the deep reality beyond the surface symptoms. The developed mind and senses can perceive this, and the dulled mind and senses cannot. This is just like knowing the speaker from the speech. The developed mind can see the author in the book and by understanding the author's personality and intentions, he understands what the book is really saying. The underdeveloped mind, however, cannot see the author in the book. He will rely on structures of grammar and dictionary meanings creating a huge potential for misunderstanding because (a) the same sentence can be interpreted as having many structures, and (b) each word can have multiple meanings.

The Problem of Deciding Meaning

A classic example of many structures of a sentence is the AI problem in which a computer is tasked to interpret the sentence "I saw a man on a hill with a telescope" which has many possible meanings—e.g., (a) the man was on the hill looking into a telescope and I saw him in that state from the ground, and (b) the man was standing on the hill and I saw him in that state while looking through my telescope. Structural variations arise because words like "on" and "with" can be bound to the seer and the seen. Similarly, classic examples of multiple meanings of words abound all over logic, set theory, and mathematics, and they lead to contradictions. To avoid these contradictions, linguistic discourse is limited to sentences in which each word has only one meaning, such that sentences with alternative meanings can never be discussed. They may, of course, be true or false. But there is no way to know that truth or falsity.

The problems of grammatical structure and multiple meanings of words preclude the ability to read and understand the correct meaning of a sentence—i.e., as originally intended by the author. Either all the possible meanings must be permitted leading us to numerous contradictions with other statements where the words mean differently. Or some of those possible meanings must be eliminated universally to create a misunderstanding of the text because alternative meanings are necessary for it. The problem of interpretation entails that the true meaning of the text cannot be known because (a) we will restrict ourselves to the surface reality, (b) we cannot identify the grammatical structure and one of the many possible meanings of words contextually, and (c) we cannot see the author in the speech so we cannot know what structure and meanings *he* intended while uttering those words. We interpret the speaker's words just as what we would mean if *we* had uttered the same sentences.

The solution to this problem requires us to see multiple levels of "deeper" realities including (a) the author, his mood while saying this, his intentions in making those claims, what he is referring to, the person to whom he was speaking at that point, and the effect intended by him, (b) the specific context of the time, place, and roles involved in the conversation, (c) the grammatical structures, (d) the nuances of culture, norms, and assumptions hidden in a language both for the speaker and the listener, (e) the nuances of the audience to whom the speaker is talking to, and (f) the specific sounds, letters, and words uttered in that speech. Each of these six underdetermines the meaning without the others. If we rely only on the "surface" reality of sounds, then their meaning is hugely underdetermined. We can know the true meaning only if we can perceive all six layers beginning with the sounds and ending with the author.

Western Neglect of Immanence

This problem of immanence is so important, and yet so neglected in modern thinking, that its true significance is hugely underestimated. The same problem appears in all experiences. There are so many deeper realities hidden in every sense perception that unless we develop our perceptual capabilities, we cannot know the reality truthfully. The simplest illustration of that problem is our inability to distinguish dreaming from waking, hallucination from the perception of reality, and the vision of truth from the vision of delusion.

These problems cannot be solved without understanding how the same thing is transcendent and immanent. For instance, if I'm seeing an apple, the apple is transcendent to me, but that apple is also immanent in the perception due to which we can know that this perception corresponds to the apple and is not a self-created hallucination. We can know that only if we can see that the sender's address immanent in the percepts of red, round, and sweet is not mine.

Immanent realities have been disregarded in Western philosophy from the outset. For example, in the Socratic allegory of shadows on the cave wall, our perceptions are like shadows cast on a cave wall but we cannot know whether those shadows are cast by dancing men or a shadowgraphist. Socrates does not consider the possibility that there is something in the shadows that could tell us about their cause. He assumes that the causes cannot be known from the effects, many causes can produce the same effect, and hence, there is no way to know which cause is responsible for producing which effect in which case.

In Humean skepticism, there is no necessity for causality because the same effect can be produced by many causes. Hume ignores the possibility that the cause could be immanent in the effect and hence even as many causes can produce an effect, in a specific case, only one cause is producing the effect.

In Kantian philosophy, there is an unknowable noumenon that creates a perceptual phenomenon and we interpret that phenomenon according to our innate mental categories—because we cannot know the noumena causing the phenomena. It is like saying that when I read the book, I cannot know the author because all I have in front of me are the words printed on paper.

In Cartesian skepticism, our minds could be controlled by an evil demon and God's benevolence rescues us from delusion. Descartes doesn't consider the possibility that there may be something within the delusion—e.g., double standards or inconsistencies—that could help us distinguish it from the truth.

In Einsteinian relativity, each person measures the same reality—e.g., distance and duration—differently due to their state of motion. However, there is no way to know which of these is the truth because Einstein insists that the observer can never know his own state of movement, and hence, there is no way to know if the observed value corresponds to a moving or stationary observer. If he had considered the possibility of immanent truth, then a moving observer's observation will include two contributor identities—of the observer and the observed—and could be rejected as the true observation. A true observation would be that which excludes the observer's identity in the percept.

In logic, set theory, and mathematics, each word can have only one meaning to avoid contradictions thereby eliminating all sentences from a rational discourse that could have relied on alternative meanings of words. Logic, set theory, and mathematics eliminate the possibility that different people may use the same words in different ways at different times, places, and roles, and by embedding all that contextual information in the sentence we could interpret the same sentence in a different way without producing a contradiction.

Rejection of Purificatory Processes

The net result of all these problems is a total collapse of epistemology because (a) either the truth can never be known, or (b) there is no objective truth, and whatever we call "truth" is simply the result of our personal beliefs, or (c) some universal truth must be forced either by God, a fixed set of rules and meanings defined by a group of individuals to preclude any alternative interpretation, or a worldly autocrat dictating rules for us. Truth is at best a mutually agreed-upon convention and at worst a coerced edict. Infinite real possibilities must be eliminated from this coerced or mutually agreed-on truth, making it not just incomplete, but also incompatible with other mutual agreements or coercions.

Due to the philosophical disregard for immanence, Western philosophy has never focused on how to enhance sensual and mental capacities. It is assumed that nobody can see more than anyone else. What they say can be accepted as truth if it matches our personal opinions. Otherwise, what they say must be disregarded as their personal opinion, unless it is dictated by institutional or dictatorial edicts. These false standards of deciding truth—that completely disregard the perceptual development to see the immanent reality—lead to arbitrary acceptance and rejection of any and all truth claims.

Some people arbitrarily accept different religious claims because it matches their personal opinions. They also arbitrarily reject different religious claims because they don't match their personal opinions. They interpret the sentences in books according to their chosen preferences disregarding the intended meanings of the author because the author cannot be seen in the book. They cannot distinguish between hallucination and reality because they cannot distinguish between what is self-caused and what is other-caused because they cannot read the sender's address hidden in the received message.

Truth is Not For Everyone

There is no answer to these problems other than developing one's perception. That perceptual capacity exists in everyone but is covered and hidden by chitta, guna, and karma. The chitta hides our ability to perceive everything. The guna creates proclivities to prioritize one reality over another. And karma restricts our opportunities to encounter some realities. For instance, if we talk about seeing deeper realities, those whose chitta is contaminated cannot see its existence and they claim that it doesn't exist. Those who are accustomed to prioritizing the vision of surface realities over deeper realities want sense-perceivable evidence for the deeper reality. And those who are inhibited by karma will never come into contact with anyone who can see deeper realities and tell them about them. Chitta, guna, and karma inhibit the truth.

Therefore, truth is not for everyone. Only those who deserve to know the truth will get to know it theoretically. Then, only those who desire to see that truth directly will practice sincerely. And only those who practice sincerely will develop the capacity to perceive the truth empirically. Everyone else will suffer before they reject their false ideas. For instance, when we apply binary logic to reality, we get probability, uncertainty, indeterminism, and incompleteness. But most people don't care about these problems as long as they are happy. When their life becomes miserable, they iterate through many solutions to eliminate the suffering. But it doesn't work due to the same reasons they ignored earlier. Misery makes a person realize the gravity of the neglected problems.

Epistemology thus works primarily by *falsification*, and rarely by *verification*. Falsification is driven by suffering. You go on suffering to eliminate the lies before you come to the truth and then you verify it. It doesn't mean that we could not directly verify it at the outset. But most people will not reject falsities as long as they are happy. A falsity becomes a problem only when it is painful. You will not mind dreaming forever if that dream is happy. You wake up quickly when the dream is miserable. Thereby, epistemology must rely on suffering, rather than merely on reason and observation. Vedic texts accept that most people come to the truth only because they are suffering. Others live with the lies until they face their painful implications. Hence, rational proofs are useful only to those whose minds have been cleansed of false ideas by suffering and they need rational evidence for the truth before they pursue its realization.

Philosophers in the West have overemphasized the importance of reason and observation while underestimating the power of emotion. You don't magically get data to be explained by a theory; you often select that data that will validate your theory. You don't magically find a rational explanation for the data; you often select a model that you like and reject other models because you don't like them. When data and theories are selected based on what we tend to like, then the only way to falsify them is to produce empirical and rational conclusions that we will dislike. A dislikable rational conclusion is the incompleteness of all mathematical models and a dislikable empirical conclusion is suffering. When these are combined, then we lose the ability to resolve the suffering using mathematical models. This is real falsification. At this juncture, people will not accept the inevitability of suffering and the incapacity to resolve it.

The Role of Science and Philosophy

Science and philosophy have an important role in convincing us about the existence of the unseen. The distinction between dreaming and waking also relies on such an unseen. That unseen is the noumena hidden *within* the phenomena. Western philosophy has mistakenly put the noumena *behind* the phenomena, making it impossible for us to see it. That conclusion destroys the need for perceptual development, and religion is reduced to blind faith in the noumenon, while science is reduced to blind faith in the phenomena. When these phenomena are analyzed using binary logic in science, then the result is indeterminism, incompleteness, uncertainty, and probability. If instead, we change the logic, then we can get to the logically necessary (although unseen) noumenon by correctly analyzing the phenomena. Then if we are interested in seeing the unseen, we can pursue the path of cleansing the chitta.

If the noumena are hidden in the phenomena, then we can try to see deeper realities in the superficial realities. Seeing the meaning in the percepts is one such depth perception. That meaning is not our creation. It is objectively present in everything. But we may not perceive it because we don't have a developed perception. We may instead superimpose our own interpretation of the text and consider that to be the true meaning. That interpretation works for some sentences in the text but not for others. But we ignore what we don't understand, or that which we find contradictory to our previous interpretations because we are more interested in self-preservation than the truth.

A true seeker tries to find that meaning by which all statements in the text will be true. As more sentences are incorporated into the understanding of each sentence, deeper and deeper meanings are revealed, although that deeper truth is present in every single statement. The attempt to see the deeper truth hidden in the superficial facts culminate in God, as the deepest noumenon hidden in all phenomena. He is the prolific speaker in all speeches, the expressive artist in all art, the emotive musician in all music, the nimble dancer in all dances, the dramatic actor in all dramas, the wise author in all books, the magnificent architect in all structures, and the creator in all creations. Everything reveals some aspect of His power, beauty, and erudition. If we know Him, then we know everything. Knowing Him is the perfection of science and philosophy.

Arthavāda—The Doctrine of Meaning

The doctrine of these hidden meanings is called Arthavāda. That meaning exists in everything, including chairs, tables, houses, and atoms. However, some of these things can reveal the hidden quicker than others. Those things are the various practices prescribed for the cleansing of consciousness. They can be bundled together into the term "ritual". The mark of a ritual is that the superficial reality has considerable resemblance to the deeper reality in one of many ways. E.g., reading a truthful book is a ritual in which the deep and surface realities are cognitively similar. Similarly, while dancing or singing in a ritual, the deep and surface realities are emotively similar. By performing these rituals, an impression of the surface goes deep into our chitta, and becomes the deeper reality. The rate at which the surface becomes the deep reality depends on us—how strongly, unpretentiously, and exclusively we desire it.

Thus, Arthavāda says that God is hidden in the ritual of chanting mantras. By performing that ritual, the chitta is cleansed, the perceptual capacity is enhanced, and we can see the previously unseen in the seen. Philosophy can logically convince us that the unseen must be hidden in the seen. Otherwise, there is no answer to questions such as knowing whether we are awake or dreaming. What is logically necessary and yet remains hidden from our vision is a flaw we must attribute to ourselves. The chitta is therefore described as the goggles through which see, and sometimes as the veil that covers our vision to hide the complete truth from us. The removal of the veil reveals the complete truth and constitutes the ultimate confirmation, but it is obtained only if we are rationally convinced that there is an unseen in all the seen, we have a strong desire for seeing the unseen in the seen, and we sincerely practice the cleansing of the chitta to remove the veil hiding the truth to help us see the unseen.

Free Will vs. Willpower

The Problem of Free Will and Its Solution

I have discussed in an article called Free Will – Self-Control vs Other-Control the differences between two distinct ideas of free will: Self-control vs. other control. The key point of that article was the conception of free will in which we are free to control others is false, but the conception in which we can control ourselves is true.

But as anyone who practices self-control or self-improvement will tell you: There are immense difficulties even in self-control. The materialist argument against free will is based on the empirically observable fact that we don't even have control over our minds or bodies.

This is where we have to draw a distinction between "free will" and "willpower". The concept of "free will", even in the sense of self-control, is alien to Vedic philosophy. The accepted concept is "willpower" and is called icchā-śakti. Like other powers, it is *acquired* by yoga practice. Everyone doesn't have willpower. But everyone can get willpower through practice.

In this article, I will discuss the differences between free will and willpower. The crux of this distinction is that we are not natively free. Rather, the material energy instigates and controls us in various ways. To get out of this material control, we have to develop detachment and then willpower. We will conclude with the distinct between willpower and surrender.

The Materialist Critique of Free Will

The materialist critique of choice equates it to *reasoning*. A simple example of such a process is that when you want to get married, you have a set of criteria such as prosperity, love, compatibility, and so on, and you evaluate each person along that set of criteria to decide whether you should get married or not. That approach is adopted even by many matrimony or dating portals that try to match couples based on their natures. Even an astrologer does something similar, although by looking at horoscopes and matching people's natures. The critic of choice argues that given a fixed set of criteria, reasoning forces you into a choice. Of course, as time passes, those criteria generally change, and you may not find your partner compatible like before. The same criteria for reasoning may now be reapplied and the result could be a couple divorce.

This critique of choice doesn't say enough about what happens when different prospective partners match some of the criteria and not others. For instance, you might have a more prosperous life through one partner and more shared interests with another. Ideally, you would like to get a prosperous life and shared interests with a partner. But if you cannot get both, then you will choose one—prosperous life or shared interests—depending on which of these you consider more important. That prioritization may be due to previous experiences—e.g., you may have seen couples fall apart because their shared interests did not compensate for poverty, or their prosperity did not compensate for their separate interests. The critic of free will says that a person's choices are rationally driven by their previously acquired knowledge.

Why the Will is Not Free

The materialist critique of choice—also called "free will"—is based on applying constraints to freedom to say that we are *not* free to do whatever we like. We operate under many—e.g., social, economic, political, biological, physical—constraints, which preclude many alternatives. Violating these constraints hurts us, and reasoning is how we try to satisfy all the constraints to eliminate our misery. However, the materialist critique misses a few things—(a) most people cannot satisfy most of the constraints most of the time, (b) they try to satisfy one or two constraints and ignore the rest, (c) what they satisfy or ignore depends on what they consider more or less important, and (d) those preferences of more or less important are arbitrary most of the time for most of the people and can be changed by choice. The relation between will and rationality is reciprocal: By will you can change what you consider more or less important and those changes will influence your subsequent choices.

The materialist critique of choice presumes the Christian idea of "free will"—i.e., that we are free to choose whatever we like. The fact is that we are not free in this way. We are constrained by material circumstances and preferences, such that every choice involves a compromise, tradeoff, and selection of one thing over another, which then leads to the famous dictum—"You cannot have your cake and eat it too". This problem of choice is called *duality* in Vedic philosophy: You cannot have everything; you must always give up something to get something else, but you can choose what you wish to gain or lose.

The Pattern of Compromises

In the book *The Science of God*, I discuss in detail 12 such choices of compromise, in the context of knowledge. Ideally, knowledge must be consistent, complete, simple, parsimonious, necessary, sufficient, empirical, rational, operational, instrumental, stable, and novel. The reality however is that when we increase completeness we get more contradictions, and when we try to make knowledge more consistent, then we get more incompleteness. We can either use a few complex concepts or many simple concepts; we cannot get both simplicity and parsimony at once. A theory that is sufficient is not necessary (i.e., it has more arbitrary variables, constants, and equations) and a theory that is necessary (i.e., has few arbitrary variables, constants, and equations) is not sufficient. What seems rational contradicts what we can observe and what we observe seems irrational. The predictions we can make are not practically useful, and what is practically useful is not predictable. When we try to attain more stability in our knowledge, we lose novelty, and greater novelty brings instability.

I imagine that we should be able to map these 12 factors to the 12 zodiac signs to talk about how each of the planets (representing different aspects of the mind-body complex) cycle through 12 factors, trying to gain something that was earlier lost, only to lose something new that had earlier been gained. I just haven't had the time to study the 12 zodiac signs enough to carry out this mapping. But even outside the consideration of these planetary cycles, we can talk about how a person is forced by material duality to cycle through choices—each time acting rationally, and yet losing something in the process.

Duality and Absence-Driven Causality

The materialist critique of "free will" is what Vedic philosophy calls *duality*—gain and loss, hiding and revelation, acceptance and rejection, birth and death, pleasure and pain, summer and winter—and there are literally infinite such compromises to be made in order to get something we want. There is a certain amount of determinism in this process because everyone prioritizes what they are missing right now over what they have, not realizing what would be lost while gaining something new. Thus, a poor man aches for the conveniences of prosperity, while a rich man aches for the conveniences of poverty.

In Nyāya, we call this the *absence*-driven model of causation. Something is missing in all material things. Factually, many things are missing in all material things. But each person feels the *absence* of something more than others based on where they are in the cycle of changes. Children dream of the time when they will grow up to have independence and money to enjoy life. Young people dream of retirement when they would be free of the responsibilities of their profession, family, and wealth creation in the youth. And the old people dream of their erstwhile childhood when they had the energy to run around.

The Machine of Absences

Choices are mostly missing as we go through this deterministic cycle due to the absence-driven model of causation because we always dream of having what we don't have or what we have lost in this cycle. We are driven inexorably by the feeling of incompleteness, inadequacy, and emptiness. Choices appear when we reject this cyclical evolution and want to *escape* this cyclical change.

Hence, Lord Krishna states in Bhagavad-Gita 18.61: *bhrāmayan sarva-bhūtāni yantrārūḍhāni māyayā,* which means "all the living entities are moving seated on the machine of māyā". The term "māyā" means "that which is not". It is the feeling of absence, incompleteness, inadequacy, and emptiness. It cycles from one kind of absence to another, in a deterministic manner, and is hence called a *yantra* or machine. But if we develop a desire to escape this deterministic cycle, then *īśhvaraḥ sarva-bhūtānāṁ hṛid-deśhe 'rjuna tiṣhṭhati* or "the Lord situated in the heart of all living entities" guides them toward salvation from the cycle.

Detachment is Freedom

What is salvation? It is the end of the feeling of incompleteness, inadequacy, and emptiness. Even if something is seemingly absent for another person, the liberated person does not *feel* that absence. He may be alone, but he doesn't feel lonely. His life may be difficult but he doesn't feel harassed. He may be disrespected but he doesn't feel insulted. Conversely, he may be rich, but he doesn't feel gratified. He may be respected, but he isn't enamored by it. He may have comforts, but he isn't relying on them. This is *freedom* from māyā. The presences and absences of this world do not affect a liberated person.

True "free will" (as opposed to the false idea of free will in which one cycles from one feeling of absence to another) in this world is *detachment* or vairāgya, by which we stop being driven by the absences and presences of this world. The term "rāga" means attachment, dependence, or reliance on something other than the self. When we rely on something external to the self, then we feel fulfilled when it is present and unfulfilled when it is absent. That unfulfilled feeling drives us to accumulate things that we rely on, such as money, property, friends, family, occupation, and so on. But all these things are temporary; if they are here today, then they will be gone tomorrow. Even when they are present, there is always something missing, which drives us to complete them, producing a cycle of change in which what we have at present may be neglected to achieve what we don't have. Then when we lose what we have neglected, we feel incomplete again. But we felt incomplete even when we had it.

The wise person realizes that we are always materially unfulfilled. We always feel that something is missing; we think that if we just add that missing thing, then we will be fulfilled. We go in search of what is missing, neglecting what is present, and we substitute one thing for another—at best. At worst, we lose what we neglect and we don't gain what we thought would be gained by that neglect.

Everyone doesn't realize this persistent feeling of absence. Even if they realize its existence, they think that the answer is to fulfill it. They don't understand that it can never be fulfilled. At best, one kind of absence can be substituted with another kind of absence. At worst, the absence will increase. We always think that if I just had this one more thing, I would be complete. Thus, material circumstances control a person's will and the materialist says: There is no free will. It is true in the sense that the living entities are roaming from one experience to another, seated on the machine of absences. The job of this machine is to keep the living entity deluded—"I will be fulfilled if I can just get that one thing". This idea of "choice" or "free will", where we are driven toward something under the influence of its perceived absence, is false because it is always under the control of māyā and overwhelmed by a feeling of absence. This is not a real choice or will, although it is the illusion of choice or will.

The Power of Will

The real choice or will is called icchā-śakti or willpower in Vedic texts. Free will assumes that we are already free, which we are not. To restore that freedom, we need the willpower to ignore the instigations of māyā, namely, the feeling of absence. The job of māyā is to make us see what is missing in every situation and make us feel incomplete. The job of willpower is to overcome that feeling.

That willpower is attained in two ways, called jñāna and kriya, or knowledge and action. The knowledge pertains to realizing how every material situation is incomplete and action pertains to engaging in those activities that will take us out of the cycle of absences. Thus, Śvetāśvatara Upaniṣad 6.8 states: *parāsya śaktir vividhaiva śrūyate svābhāvikī jñāna-bala-kriyā ca* or "The powers of the supreme are spoken of in different ways, such as self-knowledge, self-action, and self-will". The self-will is called *bala* (strength) here, so we can call it willpower. It is the capacity to choose true self-interest rather than be controlled by the instigations of externally triggered absences (produced by māyā).

Counter to the Materialist Critique

Hence, if a materialist says "we don't have free will", the counter is "you don't have willpower". The material energy controls you and drags you around like an animal tied by a rope. The goal of human life is to become free of this control. Everyone has a choice, although they might not have willpower. Without willpower, they will never be able to exercise the choice they have. It will always lie unutilized and they will remain convinced that they have no choice. Hence, there is the practice of yoga, by which everyone can develop willpower.

As we practice yoga, we develop willpower. That willpower is then used to further improve yoga, and gain even more willpower. By that willpower, we escape the feeling of absence and the delusion that we have no choice. By willpower, we can change our priorities, or what we consider more or less important. Any transformation requires willpower, and willpower comes from yoga. The practice of yoga is therefore the best answer to the problem of choice. Practice it and realize the power of will. Or, don't practice it, remain the beast for bearing someone else's burden, and think "I have no choice".

Advanced Nuances of Free Will

For those who already understand the nuances of the self in Vedic philosophy, we can talk about many different ways in which the concept of choice is used, based on two distinct descriptions of the soul—(a) divided into three aspects called *sat-chit-ānanda*, and (b) divided into six aspects called the self-identity, intention, emotion, cognition, conation, and relation. In the six-fold description, *ānanda* is subdivided into self-identity, emotion, and intention; *chit* is subdivided into cognition and conation; *sat* is subdivided into relation.

Based on the six-fold description of the soul, we use the term "choice" in many ways. First, we can look at one thing after another, and that is a choice of relation. Second, when we look at that thing, we can describe it in many ways, which is a choice of cognition. Third, we can then act toward that thing in different ways, which is choice of conation. Fourth, we have the choice of altering our likes and dislikes, which is the choice of what emotions we will feel upon cognition and conation through a relation. Fifth, there is the choice of different goals or intentions. Sixth, and finally, there is a choice to redefine the self in a new way. Accordingly, the term "choice" has many meanings.

The general principle of the six-fold self is that there are six aspects and each aspect can be dominant or subordinate. However, one of these six aspects, namely, the self, remains unchanged while the other five can change. Hence, a person maintains his identity even if they change their relations, cognitions, conations, intentions, and emotions. The most fundamental choice emerges out of the self as the ability to redefine oneself as one thing or another. That then alters the intentions, emotions, cognitions, relations, and conations.

Choice and the Self

Thereby, we can say that choice is the nature of the self. But the self has six aspects, and the choice that began with the choice of what the self should be, alters the other choices. We can say that the self is the whole and the other five are its aspects, inseparable from the self. The choice of "Who am I?" pervades these aspects. Hence, it is not wrong to say that choice can be one of the five aspects. And it is not wrong to say that choice originates in the self. The latter statement is more fundamental, and the others are less so. If we are required to provide a single definition of choice, then we can say that it is the byproduct of the self trying to define itself in a specific manner. I can define myself in five distinct ways, and these are aspects of the self-definition choice.

When the soul is covered by material energy, five of the six aspects of the self are under material control, but the sixth, namely the self picking an identity is not. By choosing a different identity, the soul can change the other five aspects. However, it is very hard to assert that self-identity if the other five aspects of the self are controlled by matter. Hence, willpower is required to assert a new self-identity (which is the same self, although defining itself in a new way). The soul is free in the sense that it can choose to be something other than what it defines itself as right now, in five different ways. But to assert that idea of the self over the five materially controlled aspects, it needs willpower. If willpower is understood, then free will is also understood, but they are not identical.

The concepts of choice, free will, and willpower are not completely different, nor are they identical. Choice originates in the self but pervades in the other five aspects. We are free to choose an alternative idea of the self, hence there is free will. However, because these alternative ideas of the self are coerced under the control of the other five aspects, therefore, one has to apply willpower to overcome the coercion. If we understand the complete description of the self, then choice, free will, and willpower will be demarcated properly.

We can rephrase willpower as how *badly* we want to be something. If we want to be something, but we are also comfortable with our current identity, then willpower is weak. The practice of yoga makes us want to be something different badly because we realize how insignificant the current identity and its experiences are and how exceptional the alternative identity and its experience are. The realization of the insignificance of the current state is detachment and the realization of the exceptionality of the future state is attachment.

Willpower vs. Surrender

Sometimes people see a conflict between the perfection of willpower and the philosophy of devotion or *bhakti* which relies on surrender to God. But there is no contradiction. Willpower is needed to perfect detachment and surrender is needed to perfect attachment. If one can perfect the surrender to God and become attached to Him, then willpower is not required. Whenever there is surrender to God, all the feelings of incompleteness and absence are destroyed. Hence, willpower is required only when surrender to God is absent.

We also speak about willpower because materialist propaganda advances the false idea that we have no free will, preempting the practice of yoga. Willpower is acquired by the practice of yoga and it is required to persist in the practice of yoga. The denial of free will, the preemption of yoga practice, and the absence of willpower are cyclically self-fulfilling prophesies. However, if the practice of yoga is perfected by willpower, then willpower is not required because there is no feeling of incompleteness. Willpower is only a temporary necessity for the soul to separate itself from the inducements of material nature. The permanent or eternal reality is the surrender to God by which absence disappears.

Reincarnation—The Most Essential Spiritual Truth

Four Positions on Reincarnation

Some religions accept a soul without reincarnation while others accept reincarnation without a soul. In this post, I will talk about why a soul without reincarnation is problematic but reincarnation without a soul is not. We will divide ideologies into four—(a) reincarnation with a soul, (b) reincarnation without a soul, (c) soul without reincarnation, and (d) no reincarnation and no soul. Reincarnation is vital to morality. Without it, people become immoral because they think that if they can escape the results of sin in this life, they have escaped them forever.

Thus, we can call the above four ideologies moral theists, moral atheists, immoral theists, and immoral atheists. I shall compare and contrast these ideologies after describing reincarnation in precise, technical, and scientific terms. We will then be able to see why moral atheists are better than immoral theists or immoral atheists. Of course, moral theists are superior to all these three. That gives us a ladder for classifying all kinds of ideologies.

The Science of Reincarnation

Life as a Constraint on Freedom

The first key statement in the Bhagavad-Gita is: "Never was there a time when I did not exist, nor you, nor all these kings, and never will there be a time when we shall cease to exist". The soul has existed in the past, it exists in the present, and it shall exist in the future. The next key statement is: "Just as the soul goes from childhood to youth to old age in this body, similarly, at the change of body; a sober person is not confused or disturbed there (i.e., at the change of body)". Given that the soul is eternal (based on the previous statement), the next statement talks about its continuously changing bodies. The "body" here includes the "mind". Just as the body is changing, similarly, the mind.

A "body" is a set of states such as childhood, youth, and old age. Each of these states is also a set of states that we call years, months, weeks, and days. Each of these states is also a set of states such as hungry, thirsty, sleepy, and active. Thus, life is a hierarchical set of sets with subsets and states. This set is fixed at the time of birth and sequenced during a life. At the beginning of the next life, another set of sets of subsets and states is fixed. The superset of states across different lives is not fixed. But it is possible to think of the succession of lives as a set of sets—each of which constitutes one life—quite similar to how we think of one life as a set of subsets of states called childhood and youth.

Since the set of states called "life" is fixed at the time of birth, therefore, things outside the set are impossible. But we can still *sequence* these states in many ways. A limited set of states in one life can be compared to a limited dictionary. At different times, places, and situations, a subset of the dictionary—akin to one page in a dictionary—is opened for a person by nature and time. We cannot step outside that page, but we can create many sentences even with a limited vocabulary. When a person goes from one life to another, he gets a different dictionary. Its pages are turned by nature and time, constraining us to fewer words, while allowing us the freedom to construct different sentences.

Hence, reincarnation from one life to another can be talked of in the same way as reincarnation from childhood to youth. The former is a change in the dictionary while the latter is the change of the page in a dictionary. When new things happen in people's lives, they say "life is turning a page". Rebirth is then changing a dictionary. This is the meaning of the statement in the Bhagavad-Gita, indicated by the terms "just as" and "in the same way". The change in the dictionary is just like the change of a page in the dictionary. Thus, the body is not an *object*. It is a *state*. The soul is the *object* and the body is a *state* and the soul moves from one state to another. If these states are sets, then the soul moves within the set in the same way that it moves from one set to another.

The Axiom of Choice in Set Theory

We can think of the "body" as a set of elements—subsets that in turn comprise individual states. These elements are not sequenced *a priori*. We can sequence a set as S1: {A, B, C} or S2: {C, B, A}. We can also talk about a set S whose sequenced expressions are S1 and S2. But we can never describe what S is, without sequencing it. Even if we draw a set as a circle containing elements, we have sequenced it from left to right and from top to bottom by placing elements within the circle at the top left, top right, bottom left, and bottom right. The mere act of describing or illustrating a set necessitates its sequencing.

Hence, the "body" is an unmanifest state of the set in which the elements are not sequenced. Whenever it is manifest, it must be sequenced. The sequencing of elements in a set is called the Axiom of Choice in set theory because there are many ways to sequence the element—such as S1 and S2 above. These sequences can be chosen, and to manifest the unmanifest set we need choice. This is the essence of the soul-matter interaction problem and its solution—(a) matter is an unmanifest set of elements in which the order is not defined, (b) spirit is the choosing and sequencing entity, and (c) by the interaction of the unmanifest set and the sequencing agency, a manifest sequence is created.

Note how different this idea of soul-matter interaction is from the mind-body interaction problem in Cartesian dualism where mind and body are called different kinds of "substances". If we liken these "substances" to objects, then the interaction of two objects requires a *force* between them, but forces can only occur between objects of the same type. For instance, in physics, mass does not exert a force on charge; only charges exert forces on charges. So, if mind and body are interacting, then they must both be similar as charges or masses, which would also mean that they are no longer different "substances".

The solution to the Cartesian mind-body problem necessitates the reduction of the mind to the body if the body is an *object*. That is not true if a momentary body is a *state* of the soul, a collection of possible states is "life", and the soul moves from one state to another to create a sequence of bodily states.

Construction of Number Theory

Modern arithmetic is constructed from set theory in which the Axiom of Choice plays a key role in sequencing the elements to create order—first, second, third, etc. The set has no notion of first, second, or third. That property is *added* to the set by the Axiom of Choice. By the addition of choice, the unmanifest becomes manifest, which means that we can count things in an ordered sequence.

The elements being ordered are called Sāñkhya which comprises 24 basic types and subtypes, which are described hierarchically as morals, identities, beliefs, thoughts, sensations, and objects. These exist as individual types of entities in the unmanifest set. However, every experience involves some combination of each type of element. The combination is a choice, and that choice is also a sequence. Choice has three components—(a) a space component that combines some of the 24 types and subtypes, (b) a time component due to which these combinations are sequenced, and (c) a person component in which the sequence of combinations is assigned to an individual as their experience.

We cannot observe the unmanifest set, although it exists, because, at the point of observation, the unmanifest becomes our morals, identities, beliefs, thoughts, sensations, and objects. Whatever we observe is the result of combining, sequencing, and owning these elements as our experience. Sāñkhya is therefore the theory of the various types and subtypes and how they can be combined to produce an experience. Since a choice is essential to combine and sequence these types, hence, the soul is the 25th element of Sāñkhya.

There are thus two notions about numbers—(a) a manifest sequence of first, second, and third as the byproduct of choice, and (b) the hierarchically organized unmanifest set of types, which are combined to produce an experience through choice. The manifest sequence of states constitutes number theory while the unmanifest set of types is called Sāñkhya. The term Sāñkhya means "that which can be counted". In contrast, Sañkhyā means "that which has been counted". Thus, mathematics studies the *result* of combining, sequencing, and owning the 25 basic types of Sāñkhya, but it remains clueless about the underlying mechanism that produces a sequenced and countable result.

Quantity is a Result of Quality

The elements of Sāñkhya are qualities, while the result of counting—or Sañkhyā—is quantity. We can also say that Sāñkhya is the *foundation of arithmetic* or counting—i.e., it explains how a personal-spatial-temporal sequence is constructed from an unordered set, or how the manifest is created from the unmanifest. Modern set theory postulates an Axiom of Choice and allows infinite sequences. It cannot explain why and how one of those infinite sequences is created. The fact is that we cannot order a set of elements that comprises *identical elements*. Each element has to be different from the other elements for choice to order them. There must also be criteria for ordering them—e.g., order things first by color, then by shape, then by hardness, and so on. Every possible way in which things can be ordered constitutes all the ways in which choice can act and the orderable elements in the set can exist.

The quantities that result from ordering are *phenomena*, not *reality*. The reality is qualities and choice. Even to explain these quantitatively measurable phenomena, we must use qualitative reasoning. Modern science has never done that. It assumes that quantity is reality and measurement of that quantity using some other quantities constitutes a phenomenon. The problem is that even the measurement of quantities involves sequencing via the Axiom of Choice.

For example, if you were given a plate of food, you can observe it in many sequences—e.g., the shape of the food, followed by its color, followed by its smell, followed by its temperature, and so on. This is because what we call "food" is an unmanifest reality and manifest phenomena are produced by sequencing aspects of reality by choice. There are infinite possible sequences because sequencing is the Axiom of Choice. Thereby, food is not an object.

It is also a set that can be sequenced in infinite ways based on our choice.

Reincarnation in Inanimate Objects

The Problem of Indeterminism

The problem of choice is not easily understood because we think of reality in terms of inert *objects*. Factually, there are no objects. Even what we consider an object is a person. A person has six aspects—choice, intention, emotion, cognition, conation, and relation. An object—such as a table—dulls the choice, intention, emotion, and relation almost completely. Cognition and conation are dulled in the judgment of truth, good, and right (intellect, ego, and morality). The five senses of knowledge and action are limited to a few types of knowing and acting. And the mind—which establishes the relation between the senses of knowledge and action—is fixed into a few nearly constant connections.

And yet, there is still a person, although the capacities of personhood have been severely diminished. We can describe an inanimate person in the same way as we describe animate persons—i.e., they perceive something and react to it. For instance, if we push a table, the table senses the push through its sense of touch. The resulting "motion" is an effect of its senses of action. The table doesn't feel pain if you hammer it; it doesn't care if you use it or not. It has no attachment to other things in a room. It has no choice to get out of the situation. It merely perceives the world and reacts to it. Thus, even an "inert object" is a person that interacts with the world through senses and mind rather than force.

The necessity of a personal model of causation is established by the *indeterminism* of causality under which the result of an action is not *fixed* because there is still a *mind* that connects knowing to acting but the connection between the two is not fixed. We can illustrate this with an example. If you have been in crowded places, you find that people sometimes bump into you. On some days, you apologize even if it is not your fault. On other days, you look at the person irritably and say: "Watch out". On yet other days, if you are pushed, you push back. This is indeterminism: The response to a push is not fixed.

The same problem exists with so-called "inanimate objects": The response to a push is not fixed. On some days, pushing a table needs more force. On other days, the table seems to move easily with less push. This is not an illusion or instrument measurement error. In classical kinematics, colliding particle behavior is always indeterministic: (a) after a collision, they can recoil in different directions while preserving their individual identities, and (b) they can split into two or more particles which can then recoil in different directions.

The Quantum Measurement Problem

This problem of sequencing is also called the Quantum Measurement Problem. It is not just a problem of atomic theory. It is seen in every moment of life. You can focus on the taste of the food more often than its color, and the "probability" of detecting the taste would be higher than the "probability" of detecting color. That "probability" is a property of the observer-observed interaction, not just of the observed and not just of the observer. A different person can prioritize the smell of the food more than its color and observation probabilities will change. Thus, we cannot talk about probabilities of observation without including both the observer and the observed. The classical physical separation of an object from its measuring instrument is destroyed by this fact, and that takes away the false idea of objectivity in science.

The reason that this problem is now unsolvable in physics is that it was never solved in set theory. Set theory assumed the ability to sequence an unordered set of elements (by axiomatizing choice) but without explaining how choice operates. The problem of event sequencing is (a) the quantum measurement problem, (b) the problem of ordering an unordered set of elements in set theory, and (c) the designation of elements in a set as first, second, and third. The problems of mathematics, physics, and life are the same problem. The underlying mechanisms of set construction, hierarchical ordering, and time sequencing involve one theory. Current assumptions in science cannot create a solid foundation for these subjects because they have been quantifying the phenomena, thinking that those quantities are reality, failing to explain the observed sequences because they require qualities and choices, and getting stuck because the alternative needs a radically different kind of thinking.

Physical vs. Semantic Information

The fact is that we cannot rationally order a sequence of digits like 1s and 0s—unless we give them meaning—because all sequences are *equally likely*. Information under quantitative thinking is defined as the *probability* of one out of all possible sequences. For instance, 'A' and 'B' have equal information because they are 8-bit ASCII characters, 8 bits allow 256 characters, hence 256 is the "entropy" of an 8-bit sequence, and the inverse of that entropy is the probability of one of these two sequences. Information is the choice that makes the probability a reality, by selecting one out of all the possible alternatives.

This is not *semantic* information because 'A' and 'B' have the same amount of information although they are not the same. According to this idea of information, the equation "F = ma" has less information than a children's storybook, because the equation has only 6 characters while a children's storybook will have many more characters. The fact that "F = ma" can describe many scenarios is not relevant because we are not looking at the *meaning* of alphabets like F, =, m, and a. To talk about semantic information, we must have the capacity to say that "F = ma" has more information than a children's storybook. We must also be able to say that "F = ma" is *one thing* although we don't see that thing with our eyes. Then, we must have the ability to say that "$d^2x/dt^2 = F/m$" is precisely "F = ma" although it looks different.

The fact is that "F = ma" is semantically not identical to "Newton's Second Law" because in the latter we have also indicated that there was a guy called Newton who invented at least two laws, under the assumption that we start counting things from one rather than zero or any other starting number. Likewise, "Newton's Second Law" is not semantically identical to "F = ma" because the latter gives a formula for computation that the former does not. By quantifying information, we lose all the essential properties of semantics—(a) the person who created it, (b) the purposes for which he created it, (c) what it means, (d) what it does, (e) what it is a description of, and (f) why it is presently used.

The Necessity of Semantics

The quantitative measure of information is not semantics. However, that quantitative thing would not arise without semantics. If there was no person to create a formula, or he had no purpose to solve a problem, or he was incapable of thinking, or he was incapable of describing reality through a linguistic system, then the formula would not appear. When it appears, we may not see all the causes that led to its appearance and may just want to quantify it, but it won't be an adequate explanation. Hence, we can measure reality as quantities but we cannot *explain* or *predict* the quantities completely. Conversely, if we describe the world qualitatively, we can explain and predict reality completely.

The fact is that the Axiom of Choice—by which we sequence letters into a specific sentence such as "F = ma"—requires all the sophisticated apparatus of semantics, such as persons, problems, goals to solve the problem, descriptive capacity, an external reality, and a connection between description and reality. The Axiom of Choice seems very simple if we don't try to explain how, why, when, where, what, and who makes the choice. The thing we call the Axiom of Choice is enormously complicated if we do. This problem comes to the fore if we neglect the mechanisms of choice and face the probabilities of occurrences. We cannot explain how a sequence occurs without explaining choice.

Repersonalization of Reality

Personalism vs. Impersonalism

Modern science assumed that the cause-effect relation is fixed in nature. That is not a fact. Even "inanimate objects" don't have a fixed behavior due to the mind. Indeterminism in science points toward the existence of a mind, which connects the senses of knowing and acting, but that causal connection is not fixed for all places, times, situations, and things. To explain this indeterminism (rather than calling it instrument error), we need senses, mind, intellect, ego, and morality even while studying "inanimate things". With that change, the difference between animate and inanimate things would cease to exist.

In Vedic philosophy, we talk about the *dharma* of fire and water as hot and cold. They are not always hot or cold because the cause-effect relation is not fixed. But they are mostly hot and cold because there is a duty-bound mind even in fire and water. If nature is impersonalized, then water and fire will not have any dharma because duty exists only when there is a choice. If there is no choice, then there is no duty and responsibility to perform a duty. Therefore, the fundamental problem in modern thinking is impersonalism: We impersonalize water and fire, then we impersonalize plants and animals, we then depersonalize humans, and finally, we depersonalize God. By such a process, the ultimate truth becomes a formula or equation rather than a person.

Science institutes impersonalism by claiming that the cause-effect relation is fixed. Religion institutes personalism by claiming that choices have no responsibility. Thereby, we get the determinism vs. choice paradox because the mind is free while the body is deterministic. Both are wrong because causal determinism is false even in the case of so-called inanimate objects and choice without responsibility is false in the case of so-called animate persons. Choices are not free because the body constrains them. The body is not an object because it is a potential that can be activated into reality through a choice.

Living and Non-Living Things

Religions that reject reincarnation have impersonalized nature and given freedom to humans. The fact is that a human is not free in the sense that these religions presume. Similarly, matter is not deterministic in the way that we have assumed. Both science and religion are false. People often ask: Can both science and religion be true? But there is a better question: Can both be false?

There is always a choice, there is a responsibility to use that choice in a preferred manner, and when that choice is misused then the responsibility reduces the choices. A table is a person whose choices have been reduced. A table can be bought and sold. A table can be used in whatever way the owner desires. A table is depersonalized by the dulling of most aspects of personhood. This dulling doesn't make it impersonal. It is still a person that has been dulled. Even when a table is purchased, some tables go to people who keep the table clean and do not cause much damage to it while using it, but other tables go to people who keep the table unclean and cause much damage to it while using it. Which table goes to which buyer is not an accident. It is also a precise science that follows the same laws as humans. Just as some humans get a good life, similarly, some tables are bought by humans who give them a better life.

If you move a table, there is a succession of bodies of a soul. The body is not moving. The soul is moving from body to body. The issues of Cartesian mind-body dualism arise from thinking of the body as an object. They disappear if the body is a state instead of object. This answer to mind-body dualism replaces *motion* with *reincarnation*. It is the motion of the soul rather than of the body.

Can You Prove Reincarnation?

Hence, if someone says, "Can you prove reincarnation?", then we could just move our hand and say: "There". The up-and-down movement of the hand is also reincarnation because both states are potentials and by the selection of one potential and the rejection of another the hand moves. The same soul has taken a different bodily form. Hence, it is reincarnation: The soul taking a new body.

The idea that reincarnation occurs only at the time of death is a materialistic idea. The demand for proof of reincarnation arises only for someone who hasn't yet solved the mind-body problem. When we solve the mind-body problem in the above way, there is no need to prove reincarnation. We can extend this point to make a more general one: Many things that we consider problems are merely problems created by our way of thinking. Similarly, many things that we consider not to be problems are the results of other neglected problems.

The problem of life-stage sequencing that Kṛṣṇa calls the soul moving from childhood to youth to old age, can also be elaborated as the problem of day-event sequencing from hungry to lusty to sleepy, and it can also be elaborated as going from taste to smell to color to shape, during a single meal. The problem of sequencing is hierarchical—(a) at an abstract level, we can talk about life stages like childhood, youth, and old age, (b) at the next detailed level, we can talk about the sequencing of days, (c) at the next detailed level we can talk about going from hungry to lusty to sleep every day, and (d) at an even more detailed level, we can talk about going from taste to smell to color during a meal.

Once we can talk about this generic problem of event sequencing, then we can talk about reincarnation in the same breath—"Just as the soul goes from childhood to youth to old age in this body, similarly, at the time of change of body. A sober person is not confused or bewildered there". Transmigration of the soul is not merely occurring at the time of death. It is occurring even while consuming a meal because there is a sequence of events and the problem of event-sequencing is how every life is defined as the succession of events.

The Possibility of Alternative Science

Modern science was created by the objectification of matter, and tying a soul (in Cartesian philosophy) to matter without explaining how the two interact. This science has failed because (a) mechanisms of choice are assumed in set theory but never explained, (b) there is no foundation for numbers, (c) we cannot order a sequence of things without qualities, (d) quantifications of qualities can never explain qualitative experience, (e) quantification is an incomplete description of reality that fails to explain and predict observations that we call indeterminism, and (f) it creates arbitrary boundaries between mind and body, living and non-living, that we can neither explain nor justify rationally and empirically.

The alternative to modern science is found in Vedic texts, in which all changes occur due to soul movement. Even if we move our hands, we select a potential state which preexisted the movement in an unmanifest form. Even if we push a table, the motion involves the senses of knowledge and action along with a connection between them established through the mind. If we don't accept personalism, then we will get indeterminism. Hence, there is no impersonal reality. There are only persons. And yet, the six traits of personhood—choice, intention, emotion, cognition, conation, and relation—can be diminished to make a person seem impersonal. This is just like we can put tape on a person's mouth to prevent him from speaking; we can tie a person's hands and legs to make him immovable; we can put a blindfold on a person's eyes to prevent him from seeing. When everything is dulled, the capacity of personhood is not reduced. However, the person is unable to exhibit the traits of personhood.

Thus, Vedic science talks about bondage—akin to tying hands and legs, applying tape on the mouth, and blindfolding the eyes. Material energy is bondage because it diminishes our personhood. We lose intellectual, emotional, relational, and perceptual capacities as a result of matter covering the soul. When the soul is thus covered, it suffers, because it has been tied, gagged, and blindfolded. Both science and religion are about the science of binding and liberating a person. Bondage is converting a person into impersonal and liberation is removing the bondage to exhibit the full personhood.

Vedic science is simply the understanding of personhood. There is a complete person with six aspects of personhood in full. There are incomplete persons with the six aspects of personhood in part. The incomplete persons are different aspects of the complete person. The complete person is the creator, controller, and enjoyer of the parts, and the incomplete persons are created, controlled, and enjoyed by the complete person. When the incomplete person wants to become independently complete, then instead of gaining the ability to display more aspects of personhood, he starts losing the ability to display the existing aspects of personhood. A person then gradually becomes an object.

Scientific Principles of Religion

Social Order Needs Personhood

Everything we do in a social order depends on persistent

personhood. While the events are changing every moment, the person who makes the choices remains persistent. If two people get married, their bodies change the very next day. But we do not dissolve the marriage because the marriage was not between the bodies; it was rather between the souls. The body changes, but the soul does not change. The persistence of the souls entails the persistence of marriage.

If we borrow money from a bank, the body changes the very next moment after the loan is disbursed. But we have to still repay the loan. We cannot say that the body that took the loan has changed after the loan was disbursed, and hence the bank must retrieve the loan from the previous body that actually took the loan. It is understood that the loan is given to the soul, rather than to the body. The loan can be used by the soul for the body. The soul could also donate the loan in charity to other souls. But he is still required to repay the loan. The lenders and borrowers are souls. They persist even if the body becomes old and sickly.

The crimes committed during youth can be punished during old age because the person is the same even as the body has changed. The criminal cannot say that the body that did the crime is now gone and the current body is a different person. We cannot evade punishments like that. Crimes are not forgiven even if a person changes their gender, gets new facial features through plastic surgery, or alters essential organs in the body through organ transplants. All these events are changes to the body and constitute event sequences. But the soul connecting these events into a trajectory is unchanged and hence it remains responsible.

If we don't have persistent personhood, then social order cannot exist. People will get married and claim never to have been married. They will work for a company and the company would not pay them, citing the fact that the body that performed the work is now gone. People will purchase property and the government will repossess it claiming that the property bought during youth cannot be enjoyed in old age because the body has changed. Someone will commit a murder and claim that the body that committed the murder is gone.

If there is no soul separate from the changing body, society will collapse. In so far as a society exists, every single person believes in the soul. We don't have to prove its existence. Just take away the property of the non-believers, dissolve their marriages, don't pay them for the work they have done, and everyone will come to their senses. They cannot live a single day without the soul postulate.

Event Sequencing Needs Morality

When choices are the fundamental mechanism for event sequencing, then the law of sequencing is the relation between choice and responsibility. We can sequence elements in many ways and they are all choices. However, we should not sequence the elements in arbitrary ways. You cannot drive a car on the road in whatever way you like. There is a right and wrong way of driving a car. Hence, one event sequence—taking the car on the wrong side of the road—is wrong. Another event sequence—taking the car on the right side of the road—is right. Event sequences can therefore be *judged* to be right and wrong.

Similarly, while speaking, there is an event sequence of words. The event sequence "The sky is purple" is false, and should not be uttered normally. While speaking in jest is allowed, jest is also wrong while others are talking in a somber mood. Of course, you may like to joke about the sky, and it may change the mood, which may then be better for the subsequent things being said. Thus, there are three ways to judge an event sequence—(a) it can be true or false, (b) it can be good or bad, and (c) it may be right or wrong. The capacity to judge an event sequence as true, right, and good determines the event sequence. Hence, the law of event sequencing is also the law of choice and responsibility.

This law can be described as moving the soul from one collection of states to another. It is the soul moving from one life to another. Everyone gets a bag of events and sequences them by their choices. Based on the judgment of that event sequence, we get a new bag of events, which is again sequenced, and judged, to yield another bag of events to be sequenced and judged. If you don't like the events in the bag, it is because of the prior choices and their judgments. If your bag of events contains what you like, that too is due to the prior choices and their judgments. Life would be perfect if we got everything we liked, and never got anything that we disliked. It depends on the contents of the bag. But since the contents are produced as a result of prior choices, everyone can get the perfect life they want. They just have to learn to sequence the events in the current bag in a way that will lawfully get them a better bag of events.

Thus, we elevate the conversation from set theory and number theory to event sequences, to the judgment of these sequences, to formulate a law that predicts and explains the event sequence, and to talk about going from one body to another as the result of the judgment of event sequence choice. The mechanisms behind this law apply to everything from eating a meal to the transmigration of the soul from life to life. In this process, we have converted the transmigration of the soul from a religious idea to a scientific one.

The Illusory Nature of Reality

When you hit a ball with a bat, and it flies in the air, the law of motion is still the law of choice and responsibility—you have made a choice to hit the ball, and nature bears the responsibility of moving the ball as per your choice. Even that "nature" is a pre-established mental connection between knowing and acting within the bat and the ball. The ball doesn't move in a fixed way even if the manner of hitting the ball is fixed, just like a person doesn't respond to a push exactly the same at all times, places, and situations. There is indeterminism even when the ball is hit by a bat. And yet, if the variation in the connection between knowing and acting is minimal, then we can think that it is deterministic. It might even work for many cases, although it is just an approximation. That model is not a universal truth. It is mostly true.

Similarly, if a ball hits someone's head, then the hitter is liable for his choices. The ball or the bat is not liable for hitting the head because they were just acting according to a pre-established more-or-less fixed connection between knowing and acting while the person who hits the ball had the capacity to judge whether hitting is right or wrong. Finally, everyone doesn't get a chance to hit a ball with a bat. Some people are too poor to have the option to play bat and ball.

Thus, we cannot separate natural law from moral law because

(a) bat and ball hitting works due to an indeterministic knowing-acting connection, (b) the bat and ball have the capacity for judgment dulled, so they cannot distinguish between right and wrong, (c) the person who moves the bat has the capacity for judgment, (d) persons are put into different kinds of bodies based on the judgment of their prior choices, and (e) those who want to enjoy enhanced capacities of personhood are urged to use those capacities in righteous ways.

If we separate moral and natural laws, then the law by which a person gets a bat and a ball would be different from the law by which the ball moves after being hit by a bat. The purchase of a ball is as much motion of the ball as the motion after hitting the ball with a bat. We cannot say that the motion of the ball—when the ball is purchased—follows a different law than when the ball is hit by a bat.

But this is precisely the type of claim that modern science rests on. Some motions of the ball are called "physics" while other motions of the ball are called "economics". Since these motions are described using different laws, the laws of physics are incapable of describing the observables of economics while the laws of economics are incapable of describing the observables of physics. Both kinds of laws are incomplete—because neither law explains both phenomena. These laws are also mutually contradictory because the laws of physics postulate determinism whereas the laws of economics assume choice.

This simple problem of choice and determinism is found everywhere in the fragmentation of motion into different theories and laws. The laws of history differ from the laws of economics. The laws of economics differ from the laws of physics. The laws of physics differ from the laws of psychology. The laws of psychology are not those of ecology. Every subject is thereby incomplete. Every subject is contradictory to other subjects because none of these laws are real. They are all *models* of reality that approximate reality in some areas and deviate from reality in other areas. Complete modeling of reality requires infinite models, along with the knowledge of which model applies to which cases. As we go down the rabbit hole of contradictory models, we find a situation in which contradictions *between* theories become contradictions *within* a theory.

For example, the description of reality using quantum theory requires contradictory ideas like wave and particle, determinism and collapse, particles that are in more than one place simultaneously, separate things that cannot be truly separated, and so on. They are all "hot ice" and "square circles". Nobody knows what any of it means. By using contradictory words alternately, scientists create the illusion of knowledge—that which can be spoken of in words has been "comprehended" although it always employs conflicting words.

The world can now be called an "illusion"—not because it doesn't exist, but because it is not what we think it is. It is exactly like looking at a rope and perceiving a snake. If there was no rope and we saw a snake, it would be called a *hallucination* rather than an *illusion*. The world is not a hallucination. There is a real world. But that reality is like a rope, which we perceive as a snake. Therefore, the world is an illusion—for most people—who don't understand reality. Of course, even the illusion often works—e.g., you can pick up a snake like you pick up a rope. If we consider the success in picking up a rope to be proof that it is a snake, then the illusion is perpetuated because we are picking up a rope but we think we are picking up a snake. The illusion is shattered when we find that the "snake" doesn't bite. It proves that it is not a snake.

However, we can rationalize it—it is a type of snake that doesn't bite. Then we find a snake that actually bites. Since we modeled a rope as a snake, we can extend the model to say: "Reality is only snakes. However, 50% of snakes bite and the other 50% of snakes do not". We can also say: "The snakes that bite are positively charged and those that do not bite are negatively charged".

One who knows the truth might say: Hey, it is not positively- and negatively-charged snakes. It is snakes and ropes. But you can object: Postulating snakes and ropes contradicts Occam's Razor—I'm multiplying entities beyond necessity. When I can explain something using just one concept—snakes—then why do I need to add another concept? Thus, we can reject the truth. And yet, we still cannot tell which snake will be positively- or negatively-charged. Our snake-theory necessitates the use of probabilities. But we are too attached to the false theory to see its problems and reject the attempts to rectify it.

Bondage and Liberation Theory

Attachment to falsehoods is called māyā. It is not merely a falsehood—which could be corrected by observing its problems. It is a falsehood that we are attached to because it serves our current purpose. Thus, māyā has three aspects—(a) falsehood, (b) attachment, and (c) enjoyment. As long as I can go on enjoying a professional scientist's job, getting paid fat salaries for spreading falsehoods, I remain attached to falsehood and perpetuate it despite its problems. Changing the theory would jeopardize my career, and invite retribution from other scientists who don't want to change. I might be thrown out by my employer. To keep my job, I must perpetuate the falsehood.

One of the effects of māyā is group-think in which a group of people thinks in the same way, and those who think in the same way group together. To think differently, one has to leave the group because we cannot think differently within the snake-theory group. Those who want to think differently leave the group and form another group. Although if not many want to think differently, then such an alternative thinking group would not be formed. Thus, those who have found the truth may try to form a group of truth-seeking people, but if others are too attached to the snake-theory groups, such a group would not be formed. The truth thus remains unpopular due to our attachment to falsity.

This is why māyā is called bondage and the truth is called liberation. People don't want to take the trouble to leave the illusion because it is serving them in some way right now. They are afraid of change. By staying attached to snake-theory groups, they survive the day and ruin their future. It takes courage to leave a group loaded with falsehoods because the majority leans toward it. Everyone likes the safety afforded by a herd. To leave the herd, one needs an extraordinary amount of courage, which most people are simply incapable of.

Attachment to falsehood is destroyed only when enjoyment becomes suffering. Pain forces everyone to rethink. Austerity is the method by which attachment to falsehood is destroyed. Thus, liberation is also called truth, and the truth is also called happiness, because once you find the truth, then you never have to perpetuate lies, never be attached to it, and never suffer due to it. Attachment and enjoyment are not self-refuted in the case of truth. Only the attachment and enjoyment of falsehood are self-refuted through pain and suffering.

Morality to Spirituality Journey

Identity of Religion and Science

We can see how every subject above has been integrated seamlessly:

- Logical Sciences – set theory and number theory
- Natural Sciences – quantum event sequences
- Life Sciences – stages of life and changes in the body
- Social Sciences – personhood, property, and economics
- Mind Sciences – creation and perpetuation of the illusion
- Moral Philosophy – moral law, bondage, and liberation

There aren't many contradictory subjects, theories, or claims. There is just one theory. We can dwell on each of these topics in greater detail, but that would elongate this article far beyond current needs. The point I wish to make is this—Everything begins in the concept of reincarnation. Consciousness is moving from one state to another by its choice. When bad choices are made, a person is bound. When good choices are made, a person is liberated. There is no blind faith. Everything can be built from simple ideas about states and collections, ordering states in a collection through choices, the judgment of choices as true, right, and good sequences, which then lead us to a new state collection.

This is how religion is science and science is religion. The words "science" and "religion" are separate in modernity but not in Vedic thinking. There is one reality, so there must be one theory of reality. Whatever cannot be unified into one theory is a falsehood. We don't talk about "pragmatic utility" because we can lift a rope, think that we are lifting a snake, and claim that the ability to lift the "snake" proves that it is indeed the snake when it equally well proves that it is a rope. The pragmatic utility only proves that the "snake" is *not* a mountain or a car—those that we could not lift easily. It doesn't tell us what it *is*. If we get attached to snake-theory, then we can spend centuries or lifetimes in falsities, updating our snake-theory with positive and negative charge assumptions to explain the behavior of ropes and snakes probabilistically because we don't have the willpower to detach ourselves from the falsehood.

The Four Principles of Morality

The law of choice and responsibility, which then sequences events, is called the *moral law*. In Vedic texts, it is called dharma-karma. It is a natural law for this world. It is also the natural law of judgment of choices. Since the principles of morality are not easy, hence, I try to briefly discuss them here. While discussing the principles of moral judgment, we should not forget that we are talking about the law of judging choices. Nor should we detach this moral discussion of judgment from the natural law based on which events are sequenced.

Vedic texts recognize four universal moral principles—truthfulness, kindness, austerity, and cleanliness. Kindness and austerity go hand-in-hand: We take austerity on ourselves and show kindness to others. Showing kindness to oneself while giving austerity to others is not morality. Likewise, truthfulness and cleanliness go hand-in-hand: (a) mental cleanliness is conceptual clarity about the relation between the self and the world, and (b) bodily cleanliness is relational clarity about our duty where we must do what is our duty and not do what is not our duty; it may be someone else's duty, or contrary to duty.

These principles are almost never consistent. Every situation demands a different type of compromise. For example, a Zen master may say: "Never argue with a fool; people will not know the difference". He has sacrificed the truth. He has shown kindness to the fool by not fighting with him. But he has renounced the austerity needed to engage in a difficult conversation. He has also sacrificed the principle of cleanliness because he hasn't demarcated the difference between himself and his opponent, not outlined the dutiful relationships, and has failed to guide him on his duty.

However, he is better than one who launches violent attacks on others because they disagree with him.

Mahatma Gandhi prioritized austerity and kindness over truth and cleanliness. His philosophy of non-violence was about taking austerity on oneself and showing kindness to others. But he neglected the truthful clarity in which the people to whom he was showing kindness were factually immoral.

The Pāndavas accepted the austerity of going into exile. They were truthful—as they had to accept the austerity after they had lost the dice game. They showed kindness when they tried to avert war—first by asking for only five villages and then by proposing unilateral withdrawal from the war to become beggars. But Kṛṣṇa reminded them that this would sacrifice the truth—that they had been promised their kingdom after the exile. It was contrary to cleanliness in which one person starts doing the duty of another, neglecting his duty, and he is neither able to properly execute his natural duty nor the duty he embraces in lieu of the natural duty. While war broke the principle of kindness, it was upheld because austerity had been accepted during exile, truth and cleanliness had to be defended, and all attempts to show kindness by minimizing the ask to mere five villages (instead of returning the full kingdom that was rightfully theirs and had been promised) had failed. Every other option required a greater compromise to more principles of dharma than fighting the war.

We can analyze everything using the lens of dharma and organize a person's actions on the ladder of the dharma hierarchy as more and less moral, even as we are unable to uphold all four moral principles simultaneously. Dharma is that which does the least violence to the four principles collectively. Violence is accepted to defend dharma—if the option that does the least violence to dharma is violence. That is not an endorsement of reckless violence. One has to consider kindness, truthfulness, and austerity as well. If the only way three principles would be upheld is by sacrificing the fourth, and three is the maximum number of principles that can be upheld in a given time, place, and situation by a person with limited abilities to do other things, then the path that minimizes the least compromise on the fourth principle is accepted.

There are universal principles, but no universal rules and

regulations or do's and don'ts. The principles are universal, the capacity of a person to do something based on his ability is individual, and the sacrifice of one or more of the principles to the least bit necessary to uphold the others to the fullest bit possible is contextual. Universality, individuality, and contextuality are thus reconciled by the practice of dharma. This is not always easy. But accepting austerity to do the best possible thing is also dharma. Ease is not a principle of dharma. Doing the easy thing while sacrificing the right thing is contrary to the principle of austerity and hence contrary to the principles of dharma.

We can reduce dharma to a rule of *optimization*—maximize the good and minimize the bad, across times, places, situations, and persons. That which maximizes the good for more time, places, situations, and persons is better. Maximizing the good for a ruler while minimizing it for others is not maximization. But if that ruler is moral, and he will in turn maximize the goodness for more times, places, persons, and situations, then based on the principle of maximization, we can also serve the ruler. Similarly, maximizing goodness for a short time, while minimizing it for a long time is not maximization. Likewise, maximizing the good for a specific place while worsening it for other places is not the maximization of goodness.

Since this rule gets complicated, therefore, dharma is transformed into sanātana-dharma—just do what will please the Supreme Lord, because that is the equivalent of maximizing the good for all times, places, situations, and persons. Dharma and sanātana-dharma are factually not incompatible. They are also not fundamentally different. They just seem different because we are not able to look into the future, we don't know everything about other places, we are not able to imagine what is good in all situations, and we don't understand all the people. The Lord is not constrained by our limitations. He knows how to deliver the greatest good. So if we just follow His instruction, we can become the instruments of the greatest good. Of course, as our knowledge grows, our rationality comes closer to God's, and we can also understand why God is instructing us in a specific way. Those who do not understand, are urged to approach a guru who does. There is no permission for blind faith.

By this equivalence between dharma and sanātana-dharma, we can say that anything that is obviously not the maximization of goodness for all times, places, situations, and persons cannot be the will of the Lord. Any ethical system that maximizes goodness for a narrow sect, for a short time, in a limited place, or for a few situations, while minimizing goodness for other times, places, situations, and persons is not the will of the Lord. This is an *objective* measure of dharma or religion and rejection of blind faith.

Two Notions of Dharma Morality

The above concept of morality is complex, so we can simplify it to *tit-for-tat*, with two aspects. First, a person should *not* do those things that he would not like to be done to himself. Second, if someone doesn't follow the above, then a person must reciprocate what he has received. These two are the rules for prevention and cure. Under prevention, we don't do what we don't want to be done to us. Under cure, we do what others are doing. The preventive rule always precedes the curing rule. But the curing rule is opposite to the preventive rule.

This substitution of dharma is not perfect. For instance, someone can endure more austerity and show more kindness than others. But by the tit-for-tat principle, he would bring himself down to the level of the person who endures less austerity and shows less kindness. In that process, he might elevate the less austere and kind person to a level of greater austerity and kindness. But he has lowered himself in the process. Tit-for-tat brings everyone to the level of the current majority—those above the majority are demoted and those below the majority are promoted. Tit-for-tat is thus restricted to a few people in a society—e.g., a nation's government. Everyone is encouraged to raise their moral standard. But those who lower their moral standard are punished by a ruler.

Immanuel Kant called the first principle a "Categorical Imperative", which means that we should only do those things to others that we can accept on ourselves in the same time, place, and situation. He did not note the second aspect of the principle where one has to reciprocate a person's crimes on them because there is no way to reform them other than by giving them the taste of their medicine. Kantian ethics remained focused on prevention and was not extended to the cure, because the process of curing involves doing those things that one would not like to do to oneself. Logically, the prevention aspect is opposite to the curing aspect. However, both are necessary.

But there is a difference between dharma and tit-for-tat—dharma is encouraging the uplift of morality while tit-for-tat is discouraging the decline of moral standards. The tit-for-tat law is implemented by nature, emulated by a government, and called the law of karma. But karma is different from dharma. This difference is explained by Kṛṣṇa in Bhagavad-Gita: "Whenever there is a decline in dharma and rise in adharma I appear to protect the saintly and sagely people, destroy the miscreants, and establish dharma". We can ask: If nature or the government is doing tit-for-tat, then why does God have to appear?

The answer is that tit-for-tat is not enough. A society of cheaters and cheated will keep cheating each other and will never become truthful. Hence, someone is required to teach dharma, not just punish people. Hence, God appears to promote saints, destroy miscreants, and establish dharma. Destruction is God's karma function, which can also be done by nature. But the promotion of saints and reestablishing the principles of dharma is a unique function that is only done by God. When God appears, He does both. In all other situations, nature keeps rendering tit-for-tat results while dharma may be rising or falling. A society must have Brahmanas who teach dharma and Kshatriyas who implement karma. A Brahmana encourages elevation and a Kshatriya prevents degradation. The former enacts prevention and the latter enacts cure.

From Morality to Spirituality

Based on the sat-chit-ānanda triad of the soul, there is a three-step process toward spiritual perfection—morality, knowledge, and bliss. I also sometimes call them relation, cognition, and emotion. The first step is that we behave perfectly in a relationship; we call this morality. The second step is that we acquire perfect cognition; we call this knowledge. The third step is that we attain perfect emotions; we call this bliss. These are not sectarian considerations. These are applicable to all souls.

In another article called A Vedic Argument for the Existence of God, I discussed the three aspects of God—controller, creator, and enjoyer. The *sat* aspect is the controller, the *chit* aspect is the creator, and the *ānanda* aspect is the enjoyer. The controller aspect of God appears as a *judge*. The judge evaluates our choices—i.e., whether they are true, right, and good—and based on that evaluation, He assigns a result. So, the law of dharma-karma is God's judging. Even if we don't know that there is a judge, if we follow the moral path, we will get rewarded. Then, when we become moral, we get a few basic insights into life—nature is not purposeless and amoral. If it is not amoral and purposeless, then whose purpose and morality are being used to judge my actions? That is the beginning of knowledge. If we don't believe that nature is purposeful and moral, then everything we create as "knowledge" will be a falsity. If one thinks that nature is cruel, evil, immoral, or agnostic and amoral, then the journey toward knowledge hasn't yet begun. That journey doesn't begin because we are immoral. It only begins when we have become moral.

The three traits of morality, knowledge, and bliss are the traits of both soul and God. Nobody wants to be treated unjustly, so everyone wants the right. Nobody wants to be cheated, so everyone wants the truth. Nobody wants to be unhappy, so everyone is seeking bliss. But we might think that we can mistreat others, cheat others, and displease others. That is an inconsistency between self and others. When that inconsistency arises, then a person must be subjected to the same injustice, cheating, and displeasure to bring them back to the situation where they are treating others just as they would like to be treated.

The Essence of Moral Religions

Vedic Emphasis on Reincarnation

The Vaishnava tradition accepts Bhagavad-Gita as the most basic text. It then talks about the Bhāgavata Purāṇa as a more advanced text. The Gaudīya Vaishnavas talk about Caitanya-caritāmṛta as an even more advanced text. This ladder is not whimsical because all Vaishnava traditions accept the Bhagavad-Gita and Bhagavata Purāṇa to prescribe Bhakti as the method for the goal of Mukti. The Gaudīya Vaishnava tradition says that Bhakti is both the method and the complete goal, and it describes advanced stages of love of God under which Mukti is rejected. That advanced stage is Caitanya-caritāmṛta. The ladder, therefore, conforms to the other schools of Vaishnavism in the first two steps and deviates in the third step by rejecting Mukti and preferring Bhakti.

Within Bhagavad-Gita, there are 18 chapters, of which the 2nd chapter is the beginning of philosophical topics. In it, Kṛṣṇa talks about the eternity and immortality of the soul. Within the 2nd chapter, the first statement is "Never was there a time when I did not exist, nor you, nor all these kings". Every soul, along with God, existed prior to this life. This is not my first life. And hence, it will also not be the last life. Thus, we start with the most basic book in the pantheon of Vedic scriptures. Within this book, we begin with the most basic chapter. Within this chapter, we begin with the first philosophical sentence about prior lives. If someone rejects the first statement in the most basic book, then there can be no further conversation. Without reincarnation, there is no concept of "bondage" (the cycle of birth and death) and hence there is no concept of "liberation" (freedom from the life-death cycle). Without bondage and liberation, there is no concept of Mukti. Without that, there is no Bhakti.

Without reincarnation, there can be no karma-yoga, jñāna-yoga, dhyāna-yoga, or bhakti-yoga. We see this in the religions that reject reincarnation. They replace duty with rights. They replace knowledge with blind faith. They reject the inward meditative journey and expound outward measures of progress. They substitute devotional love with selfish contracts. Every single form of yoga practice is thus rejected precisely as a result of rejecting reincarnation.

The Sukriti vs. Duṣkṛti Distinction

Those who accept reincarnation become moral. They know that they cannot escape the outcomes of their deeds. Even if they escape the results of deeds temporarily, those will come back to them in the next life. The simple idea of reincarnation instills responsibility in society and makes people moral. We don't need a big government to enforce laws, because most people are moral. They are moral because they know that what they are doing will come back to reward or punish them in the future. Inner drive replaces external coercion.

Moral people perform good deeds and are called Sukriti. They turn toward God in one of four ways, as stated in Bhagavad-Gita 7.16. Similarly, those who are immoral, and have performed many bad deeds, are called Duṣkṛti. They turn away from God in one of four ways, as stated in Bhagavad-Gita 7.15.

Dharma is generally done with some material desire. For example, people go to work in a job to get paid at the end of the month. In Vedic texts, we call this karma-kānda or "fruitive activity". It leads to materially good results, and the person is therefore called Sukriti. Such a person turns toward God and progresses through the paths of karma-yoga, jñāna-yoga, dhyāna-yoga, and bhakti-yoga. Those who have not done their duties properly, and have not led moral lives, are called Duṣkṛti. They can never progress toward any yoga.

When the principles of morality are followed, then a person gets a better life by the natural law of choice and responsibility. If he stays moral, he gets an even better life. In this way, one progresses to better lives, until he completely transcends an unhappy world. Thus, morality is a precondition to spirituality because unless one becomes a moral person, he will not turn to God. If he progresses into immorality, he will become atheistic. However, every atheistic person is not necessarily immoral. Just as theism is a progression of morality similarly atheism is the progression of immorality. Morality or immorality are preconditions whereas theism or atheism are their inescapable results.

The debate between theism and atheism is far less important than that between morality and immorality. Morality is the first step. Moral atheists are better than immoral theists. Kṛṣṇa calls the moral people Sukriti and the immoral people Duṣkṛti. The Sukriti turn to God while the Duṣkṛti don't. The criterion for evaluating theism and atheism is morality—Sukriti vs. Duṣkṛti.

Moral and Atheistic Religions

Every religion that grew in India, traveled to other parts of the world and was modified in some ways, was rooted in the Vedic concept of reincarnation, the power of choice to change our lives, and the judgment of choices to get a new life, completely based on natural and lawful principles. God was not essential to this scientific theory *if* we say that responsibility for choice is a natural law.

Of course, we cannot justify why such a law exists because the justification for the law necessitates God. Those who wanted such justification became moral and theistic. Those who did not want that justification—as they were satisfied with the natural law of choice and responsibility—became moral and atheistic. Theism is not tied to morality if we can accept the law of responsibility and its enforcement as a natural principle. It is necessary only if we start asking: How is this moral law enforced? Why is such a law an absolute necessity?

Buddhism, Jainism, Taoism/Daoism, Zen, and Animism are examples of moral but atheistic religions. They don't believe in a Supreme Spirit or God. But they believe that we have to live morally, in harmony with other humans, animals, plants, forests, rivers, mountains, seas, and so on. They do good deeds by helping other humans, protecting natural resources, and minimizing their consumption and exploitation. Iśopaniśad says: "Everything is pervaded by God, therefore, enjoy with renunciation, don't be greedy, because this wealth doesn't belong to you". The moral but atheistic religions don't accept God, or that He pervades everything. However, they accept the principle of "enjoyment with renunciation". Even as morality can be *practiced* without accepting God, it cannot be *justified* without it. "Enjoyment with renunciation" is incomplete without "everything is pervaded by God". When we don't have a justification for morality, then the chances of becoming immoral are high. That possibility is completely eliminated when someone has the justification for morality.

In moral but atheistic religions, unless one attains inner and outer harmony—inner harmony is the end of fear, greed, and lust, and outer harmony is the end of conflict, competition, and coercion—one is not liberated from the cycle of birth and death. Their conception of harmony is not yoga—i.e., harmony with God. It is harmony with the universe. When this harmony is attained, the miserable cycle of birth and death ends although it is not spiritual bliss. Once that cycle ends, the "self"—by which they mean the ego—is destroyed. They don't have a conception of the spirit beyond the ego. But they accept *all* material elements found in Sāñkhya philosophy from the gross body to senses to mind, intellect, ego, and moral sense. They also accept that an unconscious realm of desires, abilities, and karma causes transmigration. Their words may be slightly different. Their theories may sometimes differ from those of the Vedic system. But there is considerable overlap and agreement. Even when there are differences, there is enough agreement to bring consensus due to morality.

Therefore, the Vedic tradition exists in harmony with moral but atheistic religions. It understands that those who have morality, are not troublesome to anyone, and if they become fixed in morality, they might someday seek its justification. That search will bring them to the soul and God. There is no need to fight with them to convince them of theism because (a) they are not troubling others, and (b) they are accumulating good deeds. They may be impersonalists and voidists, but they are moral. They are on a journey that leads to theism. We may disagree with their atheism, but we agree with their morality. The person who is moving in the right direction is never decried. He is accepted although his current state is not considered the final destination. This is the basic principle of harmony between religions: They must be moral. Harmonizing with immorality in the name of harmony results in self-destruction.

Cārvāka Definition of Materialism

Classical Indian ideologies are divided into three broad categories—theistic, atheistic but moral, and immoral. The Vedic tradition is theistic; Buddhist and Jain philosophies are atheistic but moral; and materialism is immoral. Both theistic and atheistic but moral religions accept reincarnation. However, the materialistic ideology rejects reincarnation. The best-known ideologue of classical materialism in India was Cārvāka. His cardinal claim goes as follows: "As long as you live, you shall live happily. Take loans and drink ghee. After all, when the body has been burnt, where is the question of coming back?"

We can contrast Cārvāka materialism to atheistic but moral religions. The former talks about taking loans, enjoying life, and never repaying the debt. The latter talks about minimizing consumption, enjoying with renunciation, and paying back debts if not in this life, then in the next. For Cārvāka, there is no coming back after death. So, if you have taken a loan, and not returned it, then there is nothing to worry about because once you die, nobody can take the loan back from you. This is an encouragement to immorality and a discouragement of morality. In contrast, in atheistic but moral religion, you have to repay all debts. If you minimize the debts in this life, your next life will be much better.

Thus, materialism can be contrasted with other ideologies by the fact that it rejects reincarnation and endorses immorality. There is a very tight link between dharma, karma, reincarnation, and morality. We cannot create a moral society unless we accept reincarnation. Those who reject reincarnation become immoral. We can see the harmony between atheistic but moral religions and the Vedic tradition—because they are Sukriti. We can see the rejection of Cārvāka materialism as praise for immorality—because they are Duṣkṛti.

A moral atheist says—I'm not going to rely on God; I'm going to rely on myself. By such reliance, I will do what needs to be done morally and thus I will succeed. The reins of my destiny, including my salvation, are in my hands. I'm going to keep them in my hands and not rely on anyone. A moral theist says—I exist to serve God. Serving God is my moral duty. I don't expect reciprocation; service is enough. So, I'm just doing my moral duty and not expecting rewards—or salvation—in return. Finally, an immoral person wants to go on sinning. If he is theistic, then he rationalizes sins using theology. If he is atheistic, he rejects the idea of sin. Cārvāka rejects the idea of sin by saying that the universe is not a moral, just, or purposeful place. There is no punishment for sin. We can keep sinning as it has no consequences. Many immoral theists say that we cannot stop sinning but God forgives all our sins. The result in these two cases is the same—the number of sins increases, although rationalized in different ways.

The rejection of reincarnation is materialism. The distinction between sinful theism and sinful atheism is academic because the actions in both are sinful, their consequences are bad, and the reasons a person gives to themselves to rationalize sin are irrelevant. All these academic and irrelevant rationalizations of sin have been constructed after rejecting reincarnation. They are akin to Cārvāka's materialism, with minor academic and irrelevant doctrinal differences that make no difference. Religions that talk of soul and God without reincarnation are therefore materialism. They can never lead a person to morality let alone salvation. Sciences that reject reincarnation are also immoral materialism. In contrast to moral atheists, we can call them sinful atheists. Without reincarnation, there is no truth in neither science nor religion.

The Vedic tradition accepts a moral atheist (i.e., one who accepts reincarnation while rejecting soul and God) and rejects an immoral theist (i.e., one who accepts soul and God while rejecting reincarnation). Reincarnation is the foundation for both science and religion. If we take out that foundation, then the superstructure of science or religion doesn't exist. Those who claim to have a superstructure without a foundation are delusional. Therefore, an immoral science and an immoral religion are oxymorons and the debates between two different rationalizations of immorality are a complete waste of time.

Present science-religion debates wander around "Is religion false?" and "Is science true?" Some people talk about "Can both science and religion be true?" But the correct question is: "Can both science and religion be false?" We come to this question if we study Vedic texts because they begin with reincarnation. Since both science and religion reject reincarnation, therefore, they are both false. Only that which begins with reincarnation can discover the truth.

Jīva Falldown—Understanding Anādi

In Chaitanya Caritāmrita 20.117, Lord Chaitanya instructs Sanātana Goswami as follows: *kṛṣṇa bhuli' sei jīva anādi-bahirmukha ataeva māyā tāre deya saṁsāra-duḥkha.* Śrila Prabhupāda translates this verse as "Forgetting Kṛṣṇa, the living entity has been attracted by the external feature from *time immemorial.* Therefore, the illusory energy [māyā] gives him all kinds of misery in his material existence". The contentious issue here is the term *anādi.* Prabhupāda translates *anādi* as "time immemorial". Many people are not satisfied with this translation. They would like to translate *anādi* as "beginningless".

With the latter translation, we would conclude that the jīva has been in the material condition since eternity, although Śrila Prabhupāda explained many times that the jīva falls from the spiritual world. He makes this point by translating *anādi* as "time immemorial", which means that we cannot *recall* our identity prior to the fall, or when precisely we fell, but that is not the absence of an eternal identity or the absence of a fall. However, the issue of the jīva fall doesn't die, because the term *anādi* can be translated as "beginningless".

In this post, I will discuss the meaning of *anādi* and why it does not mean "beginningless" but "time immemorial". There are many other places where the issue of jīva fall has been discussed by various stalwarts, and it always revolves around the meaning of *anādi.* I don't want to make this longer than necessary by citing every case of such discussion and hence I will just focus on the above statement of Lord Chaitanya. I think we can agree that the statement by Lord Chaitanya can be taken as the most authoritative verdict on this matter.

Beginningless vs. Forgetfulness

The "beginningless" translation presents an inconsistency with "forgetting Kṛṣṇa" because it is implicit that there was a time that the jīva knew Kṛṣṇa, that he subsequently forgot, which means that the fall cannot be beginningless. If the jīva never knew of Kṛṣṇa, then the question of forgetting does not arise.

There is no such conflict between *anādi* being translated as "time immemorial" and forgetting Kṛṣṇa because the latter pertains to our *memory* of the past and not to the past. I have discussed this issue in the article The Theological Problem of Falldown, noting the difference between the *past* and *history*. Our history exists in us as memory. Chitta, guna, and karma are three kinds of histories with each jīva. These histories are continuously created and destroyed. The destruction of history is not the refutation of the past. It is merely the inability to recall that it happened in the past. The event's objective occurrence is the past, but our recollection of that event is our memory and history. History is not to be equated to the past.

Thus, "forgetting Kṛṣṇa" is inconsistent with "beginningless", but consistent with "time immemorial" because the latter pertains to our memory of history rather than the past. We could reject the "beginningless" translation on that basis, but I will keep going to identify several other nuances of this issue.

The Meaning of Anādi and Ananta

The term *anādi* is often contrasted to *ananta*. The term *ādi* means beginning or start and *anta* means ending or culmination. The prefix "an" is used similarly to the prefix "a", but the former is used when the suffix begins with "a" and the latter is used when the suffix begins with something other than "a". For instance, *dvaya* means "dual" and "a" is prefixed to it to form *advaya* or "non-dual". Similarly, *bheda* means "different" and "a" is prefixed to it to form *abheda* or "non-different". The situation changes with words starting with "a"—such as *ādi* and *anta*. Now, the prefix changes to "an". If we prefix "an" to *ādi* and *anta* to form the words *anādi* and *ananta*, the meaning is "non-start" and "non-end".

The Problem of Non and Not

Someday I want to write a book on the difference between "non" and "not", but I will be brief here. The term "not" is the prerogative of *binary logic* in which things are defined by three principles—(a) the principle of identity, (b) the principle of excluded middle, and (c) the principle of non-contradiction. For instance, it is either hot or not. It cannot be both hot and not hot. It cannot be neither hot nor not hot. These three principles constitute binary logic.

A new problem arises when we move beyond X and not-X (e.g., hot and not hot) into contrasts such as hot vs. cold vs. windy. We agree that hot is *not* cold. But how? The binary logician will say that cold is another word for *not-hot*. This doesn't work as far as sense perception goes because hot and cold are two different sensations, and it is entirely possible that one has experienced hot but never felt cold. Having felt hot, it is not automatically implied that you know what it means to feel cold, or vice versa. Likewise, not-hot can also be windy, not necessarily cold. Thus, the inversion of hot is not fixed—i.e., it could be cold and windy. Therefore, by negating hot, we cannot know what it really is.

Thus, one of the guiding principles in logic is to say what it is and what it is not. One of them is not sufficient because if you say what something is, then you haven't contrasted it to what it is not, and if you say what it is not, then you haven't said what it is. This is the property of qualities, not of binary logic. Prabhupāda sometimes explained this as "always remember Kṛṣṇa and never forget Him". The fact is that we can think of cooking for Kṛṣṇa which is strictly not identical to thinking of Kṛṣṇa. And yet, it is not forgetfulness of Kṛṣṇa. Therefore, while cooking for Kṛṣṇa, we haven't forgotten Kṛṣṇa, although we aren't thinking of Him only. This is the nuance of thinking and not thinking.

The use of "not" in logic is about the absence of a presence, but that absence can be many things. This problem is recognized in Sañkhyā to say that nature comprises three qualities, namely, sattva, rajas, and tamas, and each quality is the negation of the other qualities. Since there are three opposites, therefore, the negation of one opposite could yield either of the two remaining opposites.

The third quality of windy is neither hot nor cold. Since it is not-hot, therefore, it is the opposite of hot. Since it is not-cold, it is the opposite of cold. Since it is neither hot nor cold, hence, it is the opposite of both. The negation of a quality is indeterministic due to the presence of three qualities. If we have perceived one of those opposites, but not the other, then negation can seem deterministic. But that negation would only be true 50% of the time when one of the two opposites is involved. Since these qualities can mix, therefore, the negation can be true to various extents depending on the varied combinations.

The question is: When we did not prima facie know the negation of one quality as another quality, how do we know that they are opposites *after* we have experienced them? Why don't we say that hot, cold, and windy are just three unrelated sensations? The problem is that if we treat hot, cold, and windy as merely three sensations, then we can only use assertions (i.e., that it is hot, cold, and windy) and never use negations (i.e., that it is not hot, cold, or windy).

Nyāya Presence and Absence

A system of philosophy—called Nyāya—is dedicated to the problem of quality logic. Those interested in this topic can read the commentary on Nyāya Sutra. I will focus on the solution to the problem of negation here, which is described using two terms, called *bhāva* and *abhāva,* or *presence* and *absence.* Nyāya contends that within each presence, there are many absences that exist as a "hole" in an object. For example, hot exists as a hole in cold, due to which we can say that cold is not hot. If we have felt hot but never cold, we don't see this absence, although we could. But if we have felt both hot and cold, then we perceive the absence of one quality in another, to know that they are opposites.

The term *not* applies to the absence of a quality, but that absence can be another quality. We might not see this with hot vs. not hot, because we don't expand "not hot" into "either cold or windy". That is our flaw, not nature's flaw. Not hot is not just the absence of heat but also the presence of either cold or windy. Thus, there are two meanings of not hot: (a) it is not hot, (b) it could be cold or windy. If we use binary logic *not,* then we just get the first meaning, but not the second. Binary logic is *complete* if we take the first meaning and *incomplete* if we take the second. This is the source of confusion in logic because some people believe that logic is consistent and complete because they are relying on the first meaning. But that meaning is a set of possibilities given by the second meaning.

We can call the set of possibilities given by not hot as "one thing" to claim determinism. Or we can call it "many things" to claim indeterminism. In the former case, logic is consistent and complete, but in the latter, it is inconsistent (not hot can be cold *and* windy, which are otherwise considered mutually opposed) and incomplete (since not hot can be cold *or* windy, which are simply possibilities). This problem is detected with sense perception rather than reasoning. In reasoning, "not hot" is good enough. However, during observation, it is either cold or windy. Hence, what seems to work perfectly under reasoning, becomes observationally and empirically incomplete.

Nyāya solves the problem of negation—e.g., "hot is not cold and windy"—by saying that cold and windy are present as holes within hot, so the claim about their opposition is not merely our opinion but an objective fact of reality. It would be merely our opinion if such a hole did not exist. We may not see that hole, but only such an objective existence makes it objectively true.

The new problem is: What should we call something that exists as a hole? We cannot say it is not present, and we cannot say that it is present. Hence, we call it *non-present*. It is neither present nor not present because it is present as a hole. This hole-like presence is *non-presence*. Thus, the term *abhāva* means non-presence. We don't have a word for that in English, so we call it "absence", but strictly speaking, absence is not-present, rather than non-presence. To understand non-presence, we have to say "it is conspicuous by its absence". It is absent, and yet, conspicuous. This property of being conspicuous by its absence is what we mean when we use the term *absence*. This is also what we mean when we use the prefix non-X for any suffix. It is not not-X and it is not X.

The Problem of Unmanifest Form

Bhagavad-Gita 9.4 states: *mayā tatam idaṁ sarvaṁ jagad avyakta-mūrtinā mat-sthāni sarva-bhūtāni na cāhaṁ teṣv avasthitaḥ,* which means "By Me, in My unmanifested form, this entire universe is pervaded. All beings are in Me, but I am not in them". Note the conflict—(a) by Me, everything in the universe is pervaded, and yet, (b) I am not in the things within the universe. To resolve this contradiction, Kṛṣṇa clarifies: I am pervading everything in the universe in an *unmanifest form*. This "unmanifest form" is *abhāva* in the *bhāva* or absence in the presence. It pervades everything, and yet, it is not a presence. Hence it is correct to say that "I am not in them". Kṛṣṇa is absent in this world, and yet, He is conspicuous by His absence. However, only a rare person sees how Kṛṣṇa is conspicuous by His absence. For everyone else, Kṛṣṇa is absent.

That means—absence is not absenteeism. Kṛṣṇa is present in each soul as an absence. This absence in the presence, which we normally don't feel, becomes *viraha* or the feeling of *separation* upon spiritual progress. Due to that separation, we know "I am not Kṛṣṇa" just like we can know that "hot is not cold". But if one has never experienced cold, he doesn't know that. Kṛṣṇa is in everything as a hole. That hole has a specific form—the same form as the form of Kṛṣṇa. When the separation from Kṛṣṇa appears, then He is seen both inside and outside. Just as we can see hot and cold as opposites after we have seen both, similarly, we can see Kṛṣṇa absent in the world after we have seen Kṛṣṇa. Lord Chaitanya describes this absence as *śūnyāyitaṁ jagat sarvaṁ govinda-viraheṇa me* or "in separation from Govinda, the whole world is empty".

The real Kṛṣṇa is outside, but He is present in everyone as a hole. We can say that Kṛṣṇa is present in us in an unmanifest form, but if that absence is recognized as the feeling of separation, then we see Kṛṣṇa in us because even that hole has the same form as Kṛṣṇa although the hole is not Kṛṣṇa. Thus, if we understand Nyāya, then we can understand Bhakti theoretically. There is no need to search for Kṛṣṇa externally because He is in everyone. We have to see Kṛṣṇa as the heart of hearts by developing the feeling of separation to see Him.

Kṛṣṇa within each person is non-Kṛṣṇa. We should not call that *not*-Kṛṣṇa because it would mean that this hole has a different form than that of Kṛṣṇa. And we should not call it Kṛṣṇa because it would mean that Kṛṣṇa is exclusively confined within one person, and if that person doesn't know about the hole, then nobody knows Kṛṣṇa. The term non-Kṛṣṇa means that everyone can feel the separation from Kṛṣṇa because there is a hole in the heart of the jīva. That hole looks just like Kṛṣṇa, but if we don't care about that hole, then Kṛṣṇa is still present outside. Kṛṣṇa is inside as absence and outside as presence.

The Problem of Non-Difference

Nyāya has been completely lost at present. In this age of quarrels, binary logic has appeared as the tool for reasoning when we know that it cannot be consistent and complete. Logic is the foundation for all quarrels. And yet, everyone is convinced that logic is totally fine. They also think that an alternative to logic is not needed. This logic is always used in binary forms—e.g., 1 and 0—akin to words like "hot" and "not hot". We cannot say that "not hot" is either "cold" or "windy" or some combination of these, because that will make "not hot" undefined. When we ignore this problem and move further, then we find that logical theories don't predict and explain the world completely. We call that Gödel's Incompleteness Problem. Since qualities can be mixed, or they can be one or the other alternatively, therefore, the inability to define "not X" results in Set Theory paradoxes. It is one problem that appears in many forms because reality is three opposites and not binary opposites.

Vedānta is called nyāya-prasthān, which means that if we don't know Nyāya, then we cannot know Vedānta. Since Nyāya is unknown, hence, Vedānta cannot be known. This is why one after another many Vedānta interpretations have been authored to deal with the problems of logic. The conclusion after six such interpretations is that reality is Achintya or inconceivable because if we use binary opposites then we can be either inconsistent or incomplete. If we want to know the complete truth, then we must sacrifice consistency under binary logic. Otherwise, we must use Nyāya. Thus, I have argued for the necessity of Nyāya (which I call modal, quality, or semantic logic) to understand Vedānta.

A simple example of using Nyāya is translating *abheda* as "non-difference" rather than "oneness". Since everything is a combination of qualities, therefore, everything is *non-different* from each other: Every object is present in every other object as a hole. Binary logic separates these into *thing-in-itself* entities: One object is *not* other objects. But in Nyāya, one object is *non* other objects. In quantum physics, we call this "entanglement"—that we cannot define any object independently. We can only define quantum particles collectively. We cannot explain this problem in binary logic. This is why if quantum physics tries to explain it, it ends up using contradictory concepts like particle and wave.

Everything is also defined in a quality hierarchy. For instance, yellow is a quality, but it is defined in relation to color; color is defined in relation to sight. But what is sight? The answer is Kṛṣṇa. His sight is the definition of sight. My sight is not the definition of sight, because I am mostly blind. Similarly, His smell is the definition of smell; my smelling is not the definition of smell. Kṛṣṇa is the standard that defines everything, and progressively, everything is defined in relation to Him. Hence, when we use the term *non-different*, we mean that everything is entangled with each other because it is ultimately entangled with Kṛṣṇa. He is the whole, and everything else is a part of that whole. A table is different from a chair, and yet, because they are both part of Kṛṣṇa, therefore, they are *non-different*. Unless we stop using not, and replace it with non, there can be no scientific understanding of entanglement. Since Vedic texts use non-binary logic, hence, there is no "not". Everywhere it is "non". If we translate Vedic texts into English, almost everywhere "non" becomes "not".

Non-Beginning and Non-Ending

It was important to discuss the difference between non and not, and illustrate its pervasive importance before we discuss the translation of *anādi* and *ananta* as "non-start" and "non-end". If we don't go through this process, then *anādi* and *ananta* could also be "not-starting" and "not-ending", which is a great problem, because *not* is due to binary logic and *non* is due to quality logic.

Ananta is one of the names of the Lord, which means "non-ending". Ananta is incorrectly translated as "infinite" because infinity is quantitative and you can only visualize this infinity by imagining a size bigger than the biggest you can imagine. The fact is that we can never *perceive* infinity. It is just an imaginary construct, produced in mathematics by imagining endless sequences. Therefore, if the Lord is Ananta, and that means "infinity", then we can never perceive the Lord. There can be no Ananta deities because infinity cannot be visualized as any shape. The reason we are able to make deities of Ananta is that it doesn't mean "infinite". Rather, it means "non-ending". When we treat reality as qualities, then everything is non-ending but they are not infinite.

Take for instance the quality of color. It is not *infinite* because if it were infinite, it would just remain an imaginary construct that could never be perceived. Since we can perceive color, therefore, color is not infinite. And yet, color is non-finite, because we can never *enumerate* all colors. Thereby, we can perceive color, and yet, never fully know color because to fully know color, we must enumerate all colors, which is impossible. This is also how everything is *ananta* because it is non-finite and yet perceivable. This non-finite entity is a quality. It is simultaneously perceivable and non-finite. Prakṛti is non-finite. She can be perceived as a person, and yet, a non-finite universe is within Her.

Ananta—as the name of the Lord—is akin to the white color, which includes all the shades. White can also be perceived, and yet, it contains all other colors, which cannot be enumerated. The merger of non-finite colors becomes white, which is perceivable, and hence not infinite. We must call Ananta *non-finite* because He is neither finite (due to non-finite colors) nor infinite (because He is perceivable). That non-finite entity is non-ending. It doesn't have an end and it is not endless. The term "non" thus means "neither" instead of "not".

Similarly, every shade of color is defined by the absence of other shades within itself. Hence, if you just knew red completely, then you will know that it is not green and blue, and just by that knowledge, you can construct green and blue based on the knowledge of red. Since this principle can be applied to all colors, therefore, you cannot say that one of these colors is the "original color". Every shade of color can be used to know every other shade, so it is the starting color. And yet, it is not the only conceivable starting color, because we could also start with other colors, and obtain the same result. This is non-starting.

I can start with physics and progressively know God. I can start with biology and progressively know God. I can start with mathematics and progressively know God. This is non-starting. I have used this principle in my books in which I start with the problems in a subject, provide solutions to those problems, and show that this solution is the complete truth. I can start with any subject and come to the same conclusion because the whole truth is present in all partial truths. The whole truth can pop out of the partial truth; the partial truth *contains* the full truth, although it is not the full truth. We can keep a diamond in a box. We can open the box to get the diamond. We don't equate the two.

However, this partial subject, which is also the complete truth, is not the *historically* original truth. Historically, some subjects came before other subjects. But if we advance time by a million years and delete the history of how things were created, then we can create everything from everything else. A good example of this fact is that at present most Vedic texts have been lost due to text burning during India's invasions. But *some* texts are still left. We can create the complete Veda from these texts. If history has been deleted, then everything is *anādi*. But if history is preserved, then one thing is *anādi*. When we talk about God as *anādi*, we are talking about the temporal or historical origin. However, this origin is complete and it has produced many complete truths. After producing all those complete truths, the balance is still complete. So, temporal *anādi* is not equal to spatial *anādi*. Color is spatially *anādi*, but temporally it came after the sense of sight, and hence it is not *anādi*.

Qualitative Time and Space

Time and space are not scalars or vectors. They are qualities. Since one quality points to a more abstract quality, hence, a vector nature is created, although there is no vector. Since every quality refers to a more abstract quality, hence, there are no scalars. Thus, there are no scalars or vectors. Nothing can be a scalar because it refers. Nothing can be a vector because it is a quality rather than a quantity. Space and time are qualities, not scalars or vectors.

The implication of saying that time and space are qualities is that there isn't *one time* or *one space*. There are infinite times and spaces, each of which is defined by a unique quality. The quality of space is known as a "graha" or "house" in Vedic cosmology (which is loosely and incorrectly translated as a planet). Each graha is a different space, embodying a different quality, which is also part of a bigger space, that embodies a more abstract quality. Similarly, the quality of time is unique to each individual. My time is not your time. We are all living in separate individual times because our quality of life is different.

Everyone lives for precisely 100 years based on the count of quality atoms we can consume in one life. But because quality atoms can be lower or higher, and the higher quality is long-lived while the lower quality is short-lived, hence, everyone seems to live longer or shorter. Thus, 100 years is not about calendar duration. It is about the number of quality atoms we can consume in one life.

A yogi slows down the quality consumption to increase his lifespan. Then the yogi rises on the quality ladder to redefine 100 years—i.e., the total count of quality atoms—against a higher quality. The concept of 100 years involves atomic units with each unit being one atomic quality. In one unit of time, we consume one atomic quality, which is one atomic space. But I can consume a higher or a lower quality atom which will be longer- or shorter-lived. Hence, the unit of time for me—which constitutes the time it takes to consume one quality atom—is not the same as the unit of time for you. 100 years is about the units of qualities. They can be short-lived or long-lived, with higher or lower qualities.

All these can be summarized simply—if we indulge in a low-quality life, then we have to consume a lot of quantity. The low-quality atom is short-lived, and rapid consumption of short-lived atoms shortens the lifespan. Indulging in a lot of low-quality consumption entails quick death. But if we indulge in a high-quality life, then we can consume a low quantity. The high-quality atom is also long-lived, which means that we not only consume high-quality but also less quantity, so it will take longer to exhaust the equivalent of 100 years defined by the number of atoms we can consume. Thus, those consuming higher-quality and lower-quantity atoms will naturally lead a longer life, akin to the demigods.

Apart from the sense of duration of an atomic unit of time, there is also a quality that *sequences* perceptual quality atoms to create a life. For instance, I can give you a bag of balls and ask you to sequence them. You can sequence the balls first by size, then by weight, then by color, etc. Someone else can sequence it differently. The balls are perceptual qualities, but sequencing them in some way is another quality where size comes first, weight comes second, color comes third, etc. One type of sequence is one type of personality, and a different way of sequencing is a different personality. Each personality is defined by a prioritized order of qualities. That means—given a choice, we prefer size over weight and weight over color. This is not a universal fact for everyone. It is a choice. Thereby, we can say that time is a subjective quality of sequencing priorities and space is an objective quality to be prioritized, because I can sequence the same set of balls differently from how you sequence them.

Thus, my personality constructs my personal time and your personality constructs your personal time. You measure my activity using your time, and I measure your activity using my time. There is no meaning to "time" other than this act of sequencing. There is no meaning to sequencing other than a type of personality that sequences things differently. And hence, time is constructed by a personality in the act of sequencing. I have chosen a personality. Once a personality is chosen, it creates a sequence. That sequence is time, but it was produced by a personality, which was prior chosen by a person.

Material time began for me when I chose a personality that started sequencing quality atoms. Based on this sequencing, my personality changes lawfully—i.e., it goes higher or lower—and hence my personal conception of time changes. I get a life of a human or an ant, which exists for 100 years based on the count of quality atoms. So how long have I lived in the material world? It is the number of lives multiplied by 100 years multiplied by the longevity of the consumed atoms. There is no way to know how long that is because (a) the number of lives in the past is unknown, (b) the quality of previous lives is unknown, and (c) the sequencing of high and low atoms within one life is unknown.

Transcending Material Time

If I give up the material personality, then the *concept* of time itself changes. The novelty is that the quality atoms are never *consumed*—e.g., if I eat the food, the food doesn't disappear. The taste of food is still lingering while I am perceiving the smell of the food. If the past doesn't disappear as the present appears, then every new experience is one more layer *on top of* the previous layers. The layers go on increasing because the previous layer never disappears.

Yesterday, there were some layers. Today, there are some more layers. Tomorrow, there will be even more layers. In this way, the spiritual time *passes* and yet it does not *pass* because the materialistic idea of "passing" is that the past has ceased to exist in the present. If the past hasn't ceased to exist, and yet, the present has added some more layers, then the time has passed, and yet not. This is eternal time. We can call it *non-time*, because there is yesterday, today, and tomorrow, and yet yesterday has not "gone" today, although tomorrow is "yet to arrive". History is continuously growing with the passing of time.

Entry into this eternal time is accepted only after the material past has been wiped out. After that, there are stages in which we know that I have no past, present, or future, (called Brahman), and a superior stage in which we recall the previously created impressions of spiritual experience. Entering eternal time is not entering a spiritual world as a blank slate with no memory of the previous experience. It is resuming the addition of layers to the previous layers. This resumption to the spiritual time after a short break is just like an employee who went on a vacation and then returned after a while to resume his work. The novelty in spiritual experience is that the returning soul does not remember going on vacation, or what happened during the vacation. Therefore, his vacation is likened to the blinking of an eye, where we don't receive percepts but when we open the eyes again, we see everything as it was previously.

That duration for which the person blinks may be trillions of material years, but if we don't remember that duration when we open our eyes, then it is just a blink—a time when our eyes were closed, we saw nothing, and we were missing in action for a while.

In the normal blinking in this world, we don't forget who we really are. Therefore, the metaphor should not be extended limitlessly.

The Personification of Time

The materialistic idea of time (used in modern science) imagines an "objective truth" about what happened in the past. And yet, in that conception, the past has no influence on the present. Similarly, the future has no influence on the present. In the personalistic conception of time, there is no "objective truth" about the past. The past is only that which influences the present.

During the material journey, we may not remember our past, but Nature and Time do. This objective past is called our *unconscious*, and it exists as chitta, guna, and karma. This is the only *memory* of the past. We cannot access that unconscious until it becomes conscious, so we are ignorant about it. But the unconscious is conscious for Nature and Time. If this unconscious memory is wiped out, then even Nature and Time have no recollection of this past.

If a person is liberated, and then meets Lord Shiva, who is Time personified, then Lord Shiva is not going to think: "Oh, I remember once you were a dog". It is not that the past is in the past, and we should let bygones be bygones. There is no past and there is no bygone once a person is liberated. It never happened because nobody can remember it and they cannot remember it because the memory has been wiped out. The wiping of memory is precisely the reason that the past ceases to influence the present or the future. The eternal memory of the past is only true for the spiritual world where layers upon layers are added consecutively and hence the past exists in the present eternally.

Eternal past is a false idea for the material world because: (a) history is continuously being deleted, so there is a limited recollection of the past, (b) that recollection is based on a memory that is either influencing the present or can influence the present or will influence in future, (c) memory cannot exist without causal influence, (d) if the memory is wiped then the causal influence is wiped, and (e) we cannot claim that material journey has ended and yet the memory of the material past still exists. The combination of eternal material memory along with the ending of material causation is incoherent.

Kṛṣṇa remembers when we fell from the spiritual world because there is a stack of perceptual layers denominated with each person's identity and those layers stopped increasing for some person while they were increasing for other persons. But He doesn't remember what happened in the material world when the soul returns to the spiritual world. He is not *interested* in remembering those things either. Who wants to remember irrelevant and inconsequential facts when there are more interesting things to focus on? The impersonal idea of God remembering everything from the past denies God a choice to remember.

Impersonal Concept of Time

The impersonal idea of time talks about a past that is objectively true and yet has no causal influence on the present. It is a ridiculously unscientific idea. This unscientific conception of past history arose in some religions that called God "omniscient". If God knows everything, then He must know the past.

People don't ask: How can God remember the past, including the horrible things we have done, and yet that memory plays no role in God's subsequent attitude toward us? When we talk to God, doesn't God have flashes of recall about the awful things we have done for thousands of lifetimes? Don't those flashes of recall eternally influence God's relationship with us, because He is unable to forget the past? But making big claims and not following up with their necessary implications is the norm for some people. The absence of critical thinking has been the norm rather than the exception in many religions.

This impersonal idea of time doesn't exist in personalism, because God is *not omniscient*. He can know everything, but He doesn't want to know. He remembers things that are important for the future and forgets everything else. God is eternal doesn't mean that His memory is eternal, specifically with regard to the material world which is defined by its temporality. The idea that the past exists eternally as God's knowledge is also an unscientific idea because we cannot say something exists even if it has no effect. In simple words, God remembers the good past, and forgets the bad past, after liberation. We cannot expect God to remember the past and yet not let it interfere with His actions.

Spiritual and Material Time

Material time is not spiritual time because the idea of experience in the material world is "consumption" but it is "expansion" in the spiritual world. To understand this, we need to discuss the nature of experience.

Modern science states that when we observe something, light is "transferred" and "absorbed", and the observed reality is modified in the act of observing it. In Vedic texts, nothing is "transferred" from observed reality, but properties of the observed reality are *manifest* in our senses and the mind, as they become *unmanifest* in reality. The process of manifest and unmanifest is "consumption", but reality is a person with knowledge, who doesn't become ignorant after imparting knowledge. However, having already spoken about himself, he stops speaking. Since knowledge is no longer received, it seems that it has been transferred. For the speaker to repeat the same thing, we have to request a repetition. That request for repeating what has been previously spoken involves what we call "adding energy". It seems like lost energy because the same manifest-unmanifest process is followed during the repeat request: The energy in the requestor is unmanifest when the requested start speaking yet again.

The spiritual reality is different—the speaker can speak the same thing over and over, even after it has been spoken for trillions of years because every time it will be spoken slightly differently. But even if it were repeated exactly as it was before, there is still great pleasure in repeating it. That is the magical realization one gets by chanting the Hare Krishna mantra. We can repeat the same thing over and over, and there will be no need for silence. There is no need to pump energy into the speaker because that speech is automatically springing out—described as *svayameva sphurati*. Thus, even as knowledge is not lost even in the material world after that knowledge has been expressed, we have to add energy to the speaker to make him speak the same thing again. But energy addition is unnecessary in the spiritual world because the action is spontaneous.

Since the manifest becomes unmanifest in the material world, therefore, we can model it as the *consumption* of experience. But since it never becomes unmanifest in the spiritual world, therefore, we have to model it as *expansion*. Since nothing is consumed, therefore, there is no price to be paid in return for consumption. This means that we don't need an accounting system to keep track of who has consumed how much, and how much balance consumption is remaining in their account. Such ledgers are needed only in the material world. Science is only an accounting system in which there are debits and credits, assets and liabilities, income and expenses. We don't need that accounting system in the spiritual world because that life is not a zero-sum game in which my gain ensures your loss (due to the process of consumption).

Once we gain a scientific understanding of time, along with the distinction between material and spiritual time, then we understand that the accounting ledger is not infinite. We want to keep track of the total assets and liabilities, incomes and expenses, and debits and credits for the current year. We want to know a little less about the previous years. We are totally disinterested in decades-old details. They do not matter because they may have no bearing on the present and the future. Thus, history is wiped because that history is an accounting ledger to keep track of a person's life in this world.

Correct and Incorrect Translations

When history is wiped out, we cannot know the past. This is *non-beginning* not beginningless. It means that there is an *oldest* record in our current ledger, which we can consider to be the beginning. But it may not be the real beginning. I cannot say that it is not the beginning for sure. And I cannot say that it is the beginning for sure. When we have to insist upon "neither X nor not-X" then we use *non*. That non pertains to the beginning, and hence it is non-beginning. This is the meaning of *anādi.* It is consistent with *ananta* where I have to say "neither is it ending, nor is it endless". If it were endless, then we could never perceive *ananta*. If *ananta* had an end, then it would never be spiritual or eternal truth. For me to perceive the eternal truth, I must negate both a temporal ending and need for infinite time before perception.

Acharyas give us simple truths such as translating *anādi* as "time immemorial". That is not a dictionary translation because the dictionary was created by an Englishman who never thought about the problem of perceiving the infinite. He created a dictionary in which *anādi* is "beginningless". That dictionary is flawed, and the translation by the Acharya is correct. Everything is present in "time immemorial"—(a) the past is history, (b) it is memory, (c) because memory is lost, hence, we cannot reach into the distant past, and (d) because we cannot reach into the distant past, hence we don't know if it even existed.

The translation of *anādi* as "beginningless" is rooted in God's omniscience. It is based on binary logic in which opposites are defined as beginning and not-beginning, and even if I cannot remember when it began, there must be an objective true beginning: The term *anādi* must pertain to that objective truth rather than my knowledge of it, and hence it must be beginningless.

The Necessity of Semantics

The essential lesson of these problems is that reality is also ideas. It is not stuff, things, or substances. Past and future exist in the present as the ideas of past and future. There is no contradiction between past, present, and future because the present also exists as an idea—there is the whole idea, and part of that whole is currently manifest by time, to create a partial idea called the present.

When the past, present, and future are all ideas, then there is no problem in their interaction because they exist right now, and yet, we can distinguish between them as the past, present, and future because every idea has an associated timestamp and we just consider some timestamp the present moment. That capacity to designate a timestamp as "present" is a choice. If my consciousness moves to the idea of the past, then that recollection becomes the present due to my choice. If my consciousness moves to the idea of the future, then that imagination becomes the present due to my choice. Thus, I can go into the past and the future, just as I can stay in the present. When I go into the past and future, they are still the experience of the present. Hence, any "objective" conception of the past, present, and future is deeply problematic.

We have to define the present through choice, which means that time passes because consciousness moves. If the movement of consciousness stops, then time stops. Those who can stop that movement in this life, elongate their life, because life is a fixed number of steps, and if we don't take the step, then the steps are available in the kitty we call "life". If we slow the steps, then fewer steps are used. If we take steps faster, then fewer steps are available. The steps can be longer or shorter. This is the personalist conception of time.

In the semantic approach, past, present, and future are mutually entangled ideas, which means that my idea of the present is shaped by my idea of the past and the future. If the past idea is deleted from the ensemble of ideas, then the present and the future ideas are modified because they are all mutually defined ideas. In simple words, I see the world in a specific manner right now because that perception is influenced by my ideas of the past and the future. If my ideas of the past and future change, then my present idea changes. The past and future ideas exist as *absence* in the present, and hence I can know the past from the present, although it exists in an unmanifest form in the present.

But if the past idea is deleted from the idea ensemble, then it ceases to exist in the unmanifest form in the present, and that changes the present. Then there is the oldest idea—as far as the idea ensemble is concerned—so we can call it *ādi.* If we progressively delete the past and future ideas from the ensemble, we come to a point where there is no past and future; there is only the present. Then the present becomes the *ādi.* Such a person can be said to be "living in the present" because his consciousness never goes to the past or future as they don't exist.

The Unmanifest Form of Time

Since the consciousness can move to the past and future at any time, and that becomes the present, hence, hard and fast distinctions between past, present, and future are illusory even in the material world. They are real only in the sense that we tend to go to the past and future ideas lesser than we stay in the present, and we cannot imagine the distant future and the distant past beyond a certain limit. That limit is defined by the idea of present which has the past and future existing within as holes. If we can look into the holes—i.e., what the present is *not*—then we can perceive the past and future as well. For instance, an advanced soul can look at a person and perceive their past and future lives. That is not a fixed future. It is just what is entailed by the present.

That hole-like presence of the past and future in the present is not equally present in every person. People who have led good lives in the past, performed meditation, austerity, or scriptural study, have a hole in the present that says: The past was good. They can easily accept the eternity of the Vedic texts due to that hole. They can also accept a future in which that spiritual truth will be revived. But those who haven't meditated, done austerities, or scriptural study in the past, don't have a hole of a good past. Their prior actions and impressions exist in their present as holes and they say: The past was bad. Therefore, they never want to go to the past because think that it could not have been good.

Thus, there are people who easily accept a good past, and those that accept a bad past. This is because the past exists in the present as a hole, and we can see its form, and imagine how it was previously. But since everyone doesn't have the same hole, therefore, everyone's idea of history is different. Some people are still living in a present entangled with a bad past, while others are living in a present entangled with a good past. Some people think of the past and perceive it as bad, while others think of the past and perceive it as good. Their perception is neither an illusion nor an absolute truth. It is just their personal history.

Past, present, and future become completely illusory in the spiritual world because we can go to any idea at any time. That doesn't mean everyone goes to everything at all times. Since there is a pattern of choices, therefore, there is a sense of yesterday, today, and tomorrow. But since that pattern can be changed, therefore, the distinction between yesterday, today, and tomorrow is not fixed. This is what we call *non-time*. Factually, even material time is non-time to a limited extent because we can recollect the past and imagine the future. But it is *less* non-time because given the present, our capacity to look into the distant past and the distant future is considerably limited by our personal memories.

The Science of Entanglement

Purāṇa narrate histories in the distant past and sometimes the nature of the future. The story of Lord Rāma pertains to Treta-yuga, and is about a million years old. Present-day historians trying to construct that history imagine that this story could only be a few thousand years old because even as they read Vedic texts, and vocally support its historicity, they don't completely believe in it. In their imagination, human history cannot be so distant. This is again because their present is more prominently entangled with a *recent* past rather than a *distant* past. They perceive the present more in terms of relatively recent historical records. Since the influence of distant historical records is weak, hence, their idea of the present does not prominently reveal a distant past. Hence, even if they read that Lord Rāma appeared close to a million years ago, they reduce it to a few thousand years. In this way, everyone is constructing their version of history based on their perception of the present.

Advanced devotees can also look into the distant future simply by looking at the present because the future exists in a "seed form" in the present. Most of us cannot see it, but many people can see. For instance, the Bhāgavata Purāṇa tells us that as Kali-yuga advances, the rulers will become thieves, and people will be so distressed by their rulers that they will escape into mountains and forests to return to the hunter-gatherer type of human existence. This was unimaginable in India a few thousand years ago because the job of a Kshatriya was defined as protecting citizens from thieves. But during colonial times in India, people saw how the Kshatriyas became plunderers. Thereby, what was unimaginable in India came true. This capacity to see into the future is supposed to be a mystical power. But mystical is not mysterious. It is also a science. That is the science of past, present, and future entanglement. Those who can see the holes in the present, due to the advancement of perception, can perceive the future.

Process of Scriptural Exegesis

Thus, if we try to account for a broader set of facts about time, such as—(a) the capacity to see in the past and future, (b) misconception about the past and future based on a misconception of the present, (c) that the past and future are elongated and shortened for different people, (d) existence of some past and future changes the present, (e) when we mentally go to the past or future, they reappear in the present, (f) how different people are differently influenced by the past and future, (g) how time seems longer and shorter to different people, (h) how lifetime elongates or shortens based on the capacity to decelerate or accelerate consumption in this life, and (i) it is only through an idea-like conception of reality that we can solve the problems of past and future interacting with the present, then we can get a semantic understanding of time, and the meaning of words like *anādi* and *ananta* becomes crystal clear.

But if we try to understand *anādi* and *ananta* in isolation, or translate them based on impersonalist ideas of space, time, and matter, or rely on dictionaries created by people influenced by binary logic instead of quality logic, then we will also get false ideas. Understanding the words in Vedic texts requires scientific analysis. It is not just about reading a book and thinking that because one has read a book, therefore, they know the truth. Reading is not studying. Without a scientific analysis, there is no understanding of what we are reading.

People who read Vedic texts faithfully but don't do scientific analysis do not understand what the text is saying. They have not studied the book. All their interpretations are likely false, and contrary to other statements. A person who hasn't done the scientific analysis says: The books are contradictory. This is why Vedic texts were restricted to a few people in former times who could do scientific analysis. Even as they are spread to everyone now, the criterion for understanding them hasn't changed. Scientific analysis is still essential.

The Modern Consciousness Studies Misnomer

Consciousness vs. Content Distinction

One of the hardest problems in the scientific study of consciousness is to distinguish *consciousness* from its *contents*. In the simplest sense, consciousness is the knower, and content is the known. However, in an *experience*, we cannot distinguish the knower from the known because the two are combined.

Hence, when philosophers and scientists are talking about "consciousness" they are not talking about the knower. They are talking about "experience", which doesn't distinguish knower from known. Hence, we find the philosophy of consciousness talking about *qualia* (or sense perception qualities like taste, touch, smell, sound, and sight) although qualia are not consciousness. They are just one of the many contents. Likewise, some philosophers talk about "feelings" as consciousness—e.g., "What is it to be like a bat?" Again, they are talking about content—the experience of being a bat—and not consciousness. There is not a single philosopher who talks about consciousness *per se*, as distinct from its contents.

The Prakṛti vs. Puruṣa Distinction

The distinction between consciousness and content is made in Sāñkhya by distinguishing *prakṛti* from *puruṣa*. Prakṛti includes emotions, cognitions, and relations. Cognitions include objects, sensations, concepts, and judgments. Judgments include truth, right, and good. But none of this is *puruṣa*—the knower, controller, and enjoyer—of prakṛti. Effectively, whatever modern philosophy of consciousness calls "consciousness" has everything to do with prakṛti and nothing to do with the puruṣa.

Moreover, prakṛti is known during the states of waking, dreaming, and sleeping, while the puruṣa is transcendent to these experiences. The philosophy of "consciousness" restricts itself mostly to the waking stage and neglects the more important forms of prakṛti involved during dreaming and sleeping. Modern science further restricts the waking phase to the study of the brain—the observable correlates of private experience—akin to the observation of tears produced due to the feeling of sadness. Just as tears are correlated to sadness, and yet, tears are not sadness, similarly, the observation of bodily states during the waking experience is such a limited portion of prakṛti as to be of very little consequence.

Quantifying the Consciousness Problem

Prakṛti is generally divided into eight layers—the unconscious, moral values, ego, intellect, mind, senses, sensory properties, and sense objects. The unconscious corresponds to the sleeping state; the next six properties are present during dreaming; and the last layer of sense objects is what we experience during waking. The puruṣa is beyond these three states. Effectively, the "scientific study of consciousness" is the study of $1/8^{th}$ portion of the $1/3^{rd}$ portion of prakṛti, completely excluding the puruṣa.

Now, if we are truly interested in quantification, then each of the 7 inner layers is far more complex and diverse than the outer layer. As a crude example, various types of feelings of hurt, pain, sadness, loneliness, betrayal, humiliation, and others, can produce tears. If we see someone crying, we can know that they are unhappy. But we don't know what kind of feeling they are having to produce tears. Likewise, when a person speaks a few sentences, the things that are unsaid, but lie behind what is said, and should sometimes be inferred by "reading between the lines" are far greater than what is said.

Hence, if we speak about the $1/8^{th}$ portion of the $1/3^{rd}$ portion, we don't mean the $1/24^{th}$ part of prakṛti numerically, because the inner portions are significantly bigger. How big the inner portion is depends on how sophisticated and mentally developed a person is. There is not much to be read between the lines of a lion's roar or a goat's bleating. There is a much richer inner life of a human, and that richness and complexity grow by orders of magnitude as someone advances in internal development. The body however doesn't grow in size with mental development. The body of a mentally developed person is roughly the same as that of a mentally underdeveloped person. Therefore, if we cannot see how the inner and outer are not related proportionally, and the inner reality can be orders of magnitude bigger than the same outer reality, then we haven't even formulated a strategy for studying the inner.

The Problem Gets Bigger and Bigger

If we then include the 8,400,000 species of life found across 14 planetary systems then the diversity of prakṛti becomes unimaginable, and what people like to call the "study of consciousness" begins to seem insignificant in comparison. If we then include the varied species of life across infinite other universes, whatever science calls "consciousness" would be completely irrelevant. And yet, even this variety is still prakṛti and not puruṣa. We can begin speaking about the puruṣa only when the person transcends the dualistic experience of the material world into the non-dualistic experiences, which are infinitely greater than all the dualistic material experiences, including those of all life forms across infinite universes. These non-dualistic experiences constitute the true domain of consciousness, rather than the study of the prakṛti, let alone the outermost layer of prakṛti, on a few species, in one of the universes.

Then again, even if we restrict ourselves to humans, where exactly is the mind? Biologists now talk about a "second brain" in the stomach. Since time immemorial there has been talk of the "heart" as the seat of consciousness because brain-dead people are still alive but a person dies if the heart stops. Yoga philosophy teaches us that there are 7 primary centers of the mind along the body's spine. If science focuses on the brain, it is tapping into only one of the 7 centers. Equating neuronal activity itself to the mind completely fails to account for the other well-known and lesser-known centers of the mind.

Therefore, a huge misconception about consciousness is created when (a) consciousness is equated to content, (b) content is minimized to the outermost layer of prakṛti, (c) the study is restricted to the brain of one species, (d) on one of the planets, in one of the infinite universes, and (e) the nature of puruṣa—which is far greater than everything in the material prakṛti—is disregarded. And yet, science would have us believe that their study of the brain is the study of "consciousness". It takes unimaginable hubris in a hugely unimaginative mind to claim that the limited study of the brain is the study of consciousness.

Generalizing the Abundant Scenario

Since the beginning of modern science, the most common scenario—within our limited perception—is standardized as the cardinal case under study. Exceptions to the common case are handled by making minor adjustments to the model that describes the cardinal case. Science never takes the exceptional cases as the goals for its theories at the outset because theories are built by "simplifying assumptions".

The exceptional cases are discussed much later while trying to fit the extraordinary within the scientific conception of the ordinary. The hope is that we would be able to build a rocket by adding more gears to a bicycle. After all, there are many more bicycles in the world than rockets. Therefore, a rocket must have been developed after the bicycle, and the rocket must therefore be an extension of the bicycle.

Simplification is the method of science. Under its effect, people try to model the smallest and simplest parts of nature, and then build complexity from simplicity bottom-up. If a bicycle is the simplest thing we can find, then we must build a rocket by adding more gears to it. In theory, a bicycle can go as fast as a rocket if it had enough gears. And that's all that matters. People don't have to think that adding gears to a bicycle is inefficient. If the bicycle was built with gears, and rockets are built after bicycles, then they must be bicycles with more gears. Someone will be compelled into thinking about a rocket in a new way only if the bicycle with more gears can be logically proven to be incapable of working as a rocket.

Change Follows Spectacular Failure

The frog in the well thinks that the ocean could not be bigger than its longest jump. We cannot convince the frog that the ocean is trillions of times bigger than the well. For the frog, the well is itself the ocean. Calling the study of the human brain the study of consciousness is that frog ideology. It is not different from calling the microscopic examination of tears rolling from the eyes the study of sadness.

And yet, until the limited approach fails spectacularly, it is not abandoned. At every juncture, someone will talk about adding more gears to the bicycle. This works well for science as long as the benefits of adding more gears are financially more rewarding than the cost of the gear.

But there comes a point where the cost of a bigger gear just doesn't solve the problem because we need better roads, the bicycle has to be redesigned to go faster, the tires of the bicycle have to be changed to run faster, and the engine that can drive the bigger gear also has to be rethought. A paradigm shift then occurs because we cannot build a rocket by adding gears to a bicycle. At that juncture, decades of effort spent in building a better bicycle are ruined and people have to start from scratch all over again.

Rational and intelligent people can see that this scientific study is not studying consciousness. That they are not even methodologically equipped to do that study. But the academic system will not allow anyone to tell the truth. Even if someone tells the truth, it will have no real consequences. When intelligence is not used, then the result is the shame of spectacular failure. That hopefully brings change.

Can Neuroscience Study the Mind?

Three Divisions of Knowledge

In the article Internal, Marginal, and External Knowledge I discussed a tripartite distinction within knowledge, which I described through different names—(a) first-, second-, and third-person knowledge, (b) ideal, possible, and impossible knowledge, (c) perfect, approximate, and negative knowledge, and (d) internal, marginal, and external knowledge. In this article, I will use this tripartite distinction to describe the Sāñkhya understanding of a person divided into three parts. The first part is the mind and senses, the second part is the life-force, and the third part is the body. The body is an embodiment of third-person, impossibility, external, and negative knowledge. The study of the body can tell us what the ideal, possible, or actual states are not. However, that study cannot tell us about the possible states, the perfect state, or the actual state.

Let's begin by discussing the simple example of a pen. What we call a pen is the ideal description of that thing. However, the pen can also serve as a toy, doorstop, paperweight, ornament, and weapon. However, the pen cannot serve as a boat, car, or airplane. All of these constitute knowledge of the truth. It is true to say that the thing is not a boat, car, or airplane. It is true to say that the thing is a toy, doorstop, and ornament. And it is true to say that the thing is a pen. These three categories of true statements, however, are not the same *kinds* of truths. They can be classified in three ways as ideal truth, possible truth, and impossible truth. They are all true, and yet, they are not the same type of truth.

Knowledge Under Greek Philosophy

Modern philosophy, science, or logic do not distinguish between the different kinds of truths. Logic treats all sentences the same, regardless of whether they are talking about the ideal, possible, or impossible truths. Due to Aristotelian logic, the truth of each thing is expected to be one not many. The negative truths are accepted implicitly as the denial of everything that is not the one truth. Since there are indeed many possible truths, therefore, only one among the many truths is used by philosophy, science, and logic, which is now considered the universal truth about that thing. Someone else cannot pick another truth—even though it is true—because the same thing will now become two different truths.

Greek philosophy also modeled the world as substances, objects, or things-in-themselves. Persons were excluded from this modeling. Thereby, the mind, senses, and life-force were also excluded. The divide between first-, second-, and third-person knowledge did not exist. All knowledge was reduced to third-person knowledge, which also could not be more than one truth. The assumptions of Greek philosophy are embedded in Aristotelian logic. Under this logic, the object is given a name (identifying an individual) and tied to a concept (identifying a universal). For example, one could say: "this is a pen". It implicitly entails that it is not a toy or a paperweight.

Contradictions in Knowing the Truth

Let's contrast this idea to ordinary person experiences. Suppose you touch a hot plate and feel hot. Your first-person reality is hot. But to feel it, your body—the third-person reality—must be cold. If the body was not cold, then heat would not be transferred to the body and you would not feel hot. In this process, the first- and third-person realities are logically opposed. The body is cold and the feeling is hot. If as a result of touching the hot plate the body becomes hot then heat would not be transferred from the plate to the body and the plate would now appear to be cold. Again, the first- and third-person realities are logically opposed—the body is hot and the feeling (obtained on touching the plate) is cold.

Therefore, we cannot make a singular statement about a person—i.e., whether he is hot or cold—because if the body is hot then the feeling is cold and if the body is cold then the feeling is hot. A singular statement is possible only if we disregard either the first- or the third-person realities. If both realities are accounted for, then there is a contradiction between the two because they are logically opposed to each other. Factually, the person is both first- and third-person realities. But there is no singular and logically consistent description of that person due to the inherent contradiction between these two realities.

Reality Comprised of Opposites

Therefore, Sāñkhya philosophy describes the person in three modes called sattva, rajas, and tamas. Sattva is first-person, ideal, perfect, or internal truth. Rajas is second-person, possible, approximate, or marginal truth. Tamas is third-person, impossible, negative, or external truth. These three truths are logically opposed to each other. And yet, they are the truths of the same thing. Hence, it is impossible to understand anything under binary logic—if the thing we are trying to understand is a person with three aspects. Whatever understanding we get under binary logic requires us to disregard two out of the three aspects of the person. For example, science and philosophy elevate third-person truth to the only truth. We can call singular truth object-truth, in contrast to the tripartite person-truth used in Sāñkhya.

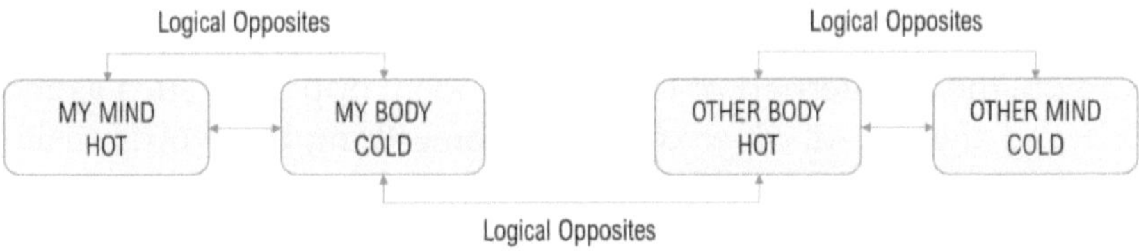

We can expand this non-binary person-truth from one person to multiple persons. For example, if I touch a person who has a fever, his body is hot, but he feels cold. When I touch him, my body is cold but I feel hot. The entire situation can be described in terms of four opposites—(a) my body and my mind, (b) other body and other mind, (c) my body and other body, and (d) my mind and other mind. The world as a whole is not consistent because there are opposite types of bodies and minds. No single thing in the world is self-consistent because the states of the bodies and the minds are mutually opposed.

The Reconciliation of Opposites

This idea is common to almost all of Eastern philosophy, not just Vedic philosophy. Material reality is described in terms of opposites like hot and cold, bitter and sweet, light and heavy, rough and smooth, etc. and is called duality (the duality is actually a triality in Sāñkhya but that is a point I have covered separately so I will not repeat it here). The two sides of the opposites are said to be mutually defined.

Buddhism calls this duality *Pratītyasamutpāda* or co-dependent arising of opposites and contends that individual things seem separate because they are results of separating opposites into different things. But these opposites can also cancel each other to become nothingness. The self and the world is one such duality. It is, in Buddhism, co-dependent arising of opposites. Duality in Buddhism emerges from nothingness and goes back into nothingness. Similarly, the world is duality in Taoism, although each opposite exists within its opposite. The opposites are symbolized as Yin and Yang. Each interpenetrates the other. The interpenetration of opposites is symbolized in the Taoist symbol of Yin and Yang.

Due to duality, Buddhists reject the idea of self-awareness because in self-awareness, the self is the opposites of knower and known, the counterpart of the co-dependent opposites such as the self and the world. How could the same thing be two opposite things? Buddhism said it was impossible. Hence, self-awareness was rejected, and nothingness was considered the only truth.

The Vedic system rejects the rejection of opposites and describes the self as three aspects called *sat-chit-ānanda*. The *ānanda* is the knower aspect of a person, the *chit* is the known aspect of the person, and the *sat* is the knowing aspect of the person. These are logically opposed to each other. And yet, they are aspects of the same person. The situation is similar to the ideal, possible, and impossible truths of the same thing. Therefore, a person can never be understood under binary logic. It doesn't mean that persons don't exist. It just means that binary logic is false. An alternative system of non-binary logic is necessary to understand persons in which one person is three logically opposed aspects.

Three Aspects of the Material Self

These three logically opposed aspects become the three modes of material nature called sattva, rajas, and tamas. They combine to form the material embodiment of a person. In that combination, the knower is the sattva, the knowing is rajas, and the known is tamas. This tripartite material embodiment of a person or soul originates in Sāñkhya through a unitary self-image of the soul called Ahaṃkāra, which then divides into three aspects due to sattva, rajas, and tamas. The sattvic aspect of Ahaṃkāra becomes the mind and the senses. The rajasic aspect of Ahaṃkāra becomes the life-force (called Prāṇa). The tamasic aspect of Ahaṃkāra becomes the body. They are three aspects of one thing–Ahaṃkāra—which is the self-image of a person. By this tripartite division, a person comes to see himself in three ways—internal, marginal, and external.

Suppose we look at ourself in a mirror and see shape, size, and color. This perception is the internal reality private to us. Corresponding to internal reality, there is an external reality which we call the thing being seen, which embodies the properties that we see, but which exists objectively even if we don't see it. Apart from these two visions, there is a third sense in which we can feel our body from within, which is neither shape, size, and color, nor the external objective reality. We think we are inside a body because we can feel the body from inside in addition to seeing it in a mirror. What we feel from within, our sensations and thoughts, and the reality corresponding to it are three aspects of our existence.

Neither Identical Nor Separate Truths

Modern science reduces the three aspects of our existence to just one—the externally observable third-person picture. That is because since Greek times, reality in the West has been studied as objects and substances, not persons. The internal and marginal realities of a person are ignored by modern science. The external reality is considered the sole truth. Thus, neuroscientists set out to study the internal and marginal realities through the external reality although everyone can see that a neuroscientist will never explain the experience of the sensations, thoughts, or the private experience of the body. For example, a scientist can measure the body state but that state will never be the experience of pleasure or pain.

Of course, it is true that every first-person experience has something corresponding in the third-person experience. For instance, when a person feels angry, his blood pressure may rise. But anger is not blood pressure. These two are neither completely independent nor are they completely identical. Modern science does not have a system of logic to deal with a reality in which two things that are neither separate nor identical. The three modes of material nature are the essential conceptual framework for such a reality. They are neither independent nor identical truths. For example, pen and not-car are neither independent nor separate truths. They are not independent because they are truths about the same thing. They are not identical because the pen is a positive truth and not-car is the negative truth of the same thing.

Entanglement of Three Aspects

An ink pen with its cap removed is not a toy as it will spill ink. We can still use it as a paperweight. An ink pen is not a weapon if its cap is on. We can still use it as a paperweight. Therefore, the possible states of something change as we make modifications to that thing. The impossible can become possible and the possible can become impossible. The internal, marginal, and external ideas of something coevolve. Therefore, the ideal, possible, and impossible truths are mutually entangled and not mutually separable.

Similarly, the internal, marginal, and external aspects of a person are entangled due to which when the senses have a first-person sensation, there is a corresponding third-person change in the body. That change is just like removing the pen's cap to convert it into a weapon when it was not earlier a weapon. Or, that restoring the pen's cap to convert it into a toy when it was not previously a toy. The negative claims about something keep changing just as we change the positive claims and vice versa. We cannot always change the negative and positive claims independently. Those claims are mutually entangled. We also cannot equate the negative and positive claims. Those claims are indeed quite different.

Thus, first-person reality is neither identical to nor independent from the third-person reality. For example, our vision will create changes in the brain and changes in the brain will create vision. That doesn't mean the vision is changes in the brain. It also doesn't mean that these two are mutually independent. They are mutually entangled as negative and positive claims, both true, and yet not the same kind of truth. We cannot explain this fact without invoking the non-binary way of thinking found in Sāñkhya.

Three Kinds of Mind-Body Theories

There are two kinds of mind-body theories at present. Mind-Body Dualism says that mind and body are two disparate things. Mind-Body Identity says that mind and body are identical. Both positions are false. Dualism is false because changes in the mind cause changes in the brain. Identity is false because brain change is not sensation. The opposition between these two false positions leads to many debates.

The Sāñkhya position can instead be called Mind-Body Non-Dualism. It means that mind and body are neither identical nor separate. We cannot articulate this idea in binary logic. We have to think of reality as knowledge, divide knowledge into three components (internal, marginal, and external), show how these three types of knowledge are neither separate nor identical, before we can talk about Mind-Body Non-Dualism. We have to also start describing a person in terms of three aspects before the relation between mind and body can be understood correctly. With that change, everything becomes easy.

The word I is not such a simple world. It comprises three components—knower, known, and knowing. They are neither identical nor separable. When I is transformed into Ahaṃkāra, or the self-image, the same tripartite distinction appears. From this self-image, expand the knower, known, and knowing aspects of the I. They become the mind and senses, the body, and the life-force, respectively.

If this tripartite nature of the I is not understood, then nothing else can be understood. Mind-Body Dualism and Mind-Body Identity are the results of not understanding the I, applying Aristotelian logic to a person (although it only applies to objects), and concluding that two things must either be identical or separate. A position that is neither of these two extremes (and yet both of these extremes) is eliminated by the use of binary logic.

Dissolution of the Mind-Body Dualism

Our senses are capable of infinite types of perception. But the body limits those perceptions to fewer percepts during waking when we interact with things at a given time, place, and situation. That limitation is removed during dreaming; then, we can see what we could not see during waking. Similarly, our minds can think infinite types of thoughts. But the body limits the possible thoughts during waking. That limit is removed during the dreaming or imaginative states; then we can think what we could not think while looking at the world. Therefore, the body acts as a filter on the mind and senses. When the mind and senses are confined to a body, a person cannot perceive or conceive all that the senses and the mind are capable of. The body reduces the sensations and thoughts to a fewer percepts and concepts.

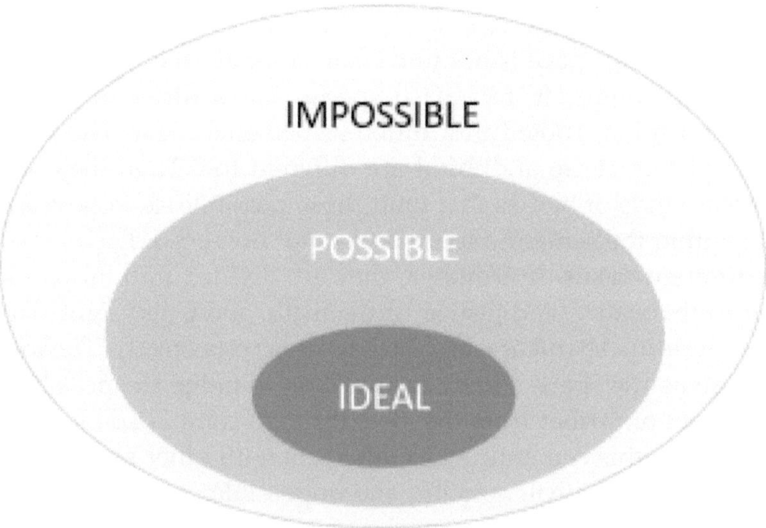

To understand this idea better, think of the senses and the mind as semantic spaces with one origin. The origin of the space is the ideal or perfect sensations or thoughts. Other sensations and thoughts are possible, but not ideal. Now imagine that this space is covered by negations that reduce the possibilities in the space to a smaller subset. Due to the negations, all that was earlier possible is not so anymore. By choice, we can still select and activate one of the many possibilities although not the impossibility.

Note how the semantic space dissolves the mind-body dualism without removing mind and body or reducing them to just one type of thing. There are still two realities—possibility and impossibility. But they are not two substances. They are also not identical. If we describe them as allowed and disallowed meanings, then we can conceptualize both as ideas, meanings, or knowledge. However, it requires us to say that the body is negative claims about what is possible. They filter or reduce possibilities. It also requires us to say that the body is nothing more than negative ideas, meanings, or knowledge.

Personalization of Material Reality

The semantic space is not universal. After all, there are infinite senses and minds. In fact, each species has a different kind of sense and mind, rooted in a different personal ideal. The possibilities of that sense and mind are different too. Then they have different kinds of bodies that limit those possibilities in turn. The ideal within the semantic space is also not universal. Each person has different ideals. In Sāñkhya, they are divided into three—the ideal truth, beauty, and justice, or the truth, good, and right—and called Buddhi, Ahaṃkāra, and Mahattattva respectively. The ideal in the semantic space allows each person to judge the possibility to be closer or farther from the ideal through comparison with the ideal. When this semantic space interacts with other spaces, they too comprise the ideal, possible, and impossible.

In this interaction between an observer and reality, the impossible component of reality applies a constraint on the observer's ideas by indicating what it is not. Many alternatives are possible even after this limitation. The observer chooses one among those based on its ideals. This is the interpretation of reality, which may not be the ideal state of reality. The ideal state may be a pen, but the interpretation may be a toy. Perception does not guarantee perfection due to the possibility of personal interpretation. Since both reality and its interpretation are semantic spaces, therefore, reality must be personalized. Space and time are not impersonal containers. They are the senses and the mind of a person. There are many spaces and times, one for each person. Therefore, personalization doesn't become Solipsism.

Multiple Conceptions of the Body

The sense-perceivable part called the body has been depersonalized as substance, object, or thing in Western thinking. Unlike a person who has will, intention, emotion, cognition, conation, and relation, a substance, object, or thing is considered dead or inert. That, however, is not the way in which Sāñkhya describes the sense-perceivable part called the five Mahābhūta (Earth, Water, Fire, Air, and Ether), that create effects of smell, taste, sight, touch, and sound in the senses. The Mahābhūta have the properties of a person—will, intention, emotion, cognition, conation, and relation—in a diminished state.

The conation of Mahābhūta is seen when they generate other Mahābhūta. The cognition of Mahābhūta is seen when they absorb other Mahābhūta. The relation of Mahābhūta is seen when they hide and reveal properties in relation to other Mahābhūta. The will of Mahābhūta is seen when they selectively interact with other Mahābhūta. The intention of Mahābhūta is seen when they self-correct, self-defend, and self-repair. The emotion of Mahābhūta is seen when they generate pleasure and pain. Due to these properties, we call a body comprising Mahābhūta an organism even if it is not sensing or thinking.

Therefore, the modeling of Mahābhūta as inanimate objects driven by mathematical formulae is grossly incorrect. The body must be modeled as filters on the senses and the mind that limit the sensual and mental capacity. In this sense, the body constitutes the impossible. The body embodies the opposite of what is in the senses and the mind. In this sense, it is negations. Unlike the subjective reality of the senses and the mind, the body is objective reality. In that sense, it is third-person. In contrast to the private experience of the senses and the mind, the body is public. In that sense, the body is external.

The Value of the Negative Conception

A sick person either hallucinates or misperceives reality. A sick person either cannot understand the true nature of the world or misunderstands it. A sick person cannot work as effectively and efficiently as a healthy person. Hence, a healthy body is desirable over a sick body. But even a healthy body disables certain kinds of thoughts and perceptions. Hence, even a healthy body is like a sickness. When that body becomes sick, the situation worsens, because some earlier sense-mind possibilities are disabled.

The study of the body is valuable in the sense that we don't want sickness. We want to operate at the fullest mental and sensual capacity that we can in this body. But the body can never become the focus of our existence because it is ultimately a sickness that disables the sensual and mental capacities.

But we cannot use bodily similarities to postulate similarities between various species because the bodily similarity just tells us what is impossible and not what is ideal or actual. For example, humans and apes have many bodily similarities. Biology elevates the similarity to say that humans are just like apes. This is not true. Humans and apes do not have the same ideals. Humans idolize art, poetry, literature, science, discovery, invention, and progress, but apes do not. Many apes have human like capacities but they don't use them because their ideals are different. Trying to teach an ape reading and writing is just as hard as trying to teach a human with no interest in reading and writing. Even humans that look similar to each other don't always have the same ideals. Body similarity doesn't indicate mind similarity.

Misconception Regarding the Body

Owing to the history of thinking about matter as substance, object, or thing, modern science cannot understand how the body is an organism. Thus, it has no capacity to explain the generative, defensive, and corrective abilities in the body. Because of elevating the body to positive truths, modern science has no capacity to integrate another kind of truth that is not sense perceivable. Thus, science has no capacity to understand the first-person experience. Since modern science models the world as physical particles rather than entangled knowledge, therefore, it has no ability to explain how changes to the mind become changes to the body and vice versa. As a combined result of these three presuppositions, neither mind-body dualism nor mind-body identity are complete scientific models of mind-body.

All these problems begin from the presupposition that the body can be studied after disregarding the senses and the mind. The mathematization of reality and the foundation of mathematics in axiomatic reasoning systems makes it impossible to understand how reality has self-defending, self-correcting, and self-generating capacities. These problems cannot be solved by adding a subject called neuroscience to the rest of science. The solution requires us to rethink the foundational presuppositions of science.

Modern science is not going to rethink those presuppositions.

The prestige tied to modern science will be defended at all costs. Of course, the cost of defending that prestige will rise continuously because every proposal will be refuted by some facts, new proposals will be harder to come by, and the cost of those new proposals will be higher. As an increasing amount of money is poured to defend the prestige of science, the return on investment in science will keep declining. This is sometimes called the Law of Diminishing Returns. A good idea has increasing returns. A bad idea has diminishing returns. The bad idea dies not because its proponents accept their mistake. It dies because the proponents run out of money to pay for defense. When the power of science comes not from the truth but from its capacity to fuel economics, then the falsification of science also comes precisely due to economic factors.

Does Consciousness Control Matter?

The Misconception of Control

There is a common misconception about the soul controlling matter. The fact is that most of us have no volitional control over our bodies and minds. We don't control our blood circulation, digestion, or neural activity in the brain. Anyone who has tried to control the mind meets with great difficulties, and concludes that the mind is not controllable. This leads many to suppose that we have no free will. That we are living in a simulation, controlled by some gigantic computer producing our experience.

And yet, there are yogic practices by which we can gradually gain control over the mind and body. While we, indeed, have no volitional control over most bodily and mental activities, we can control some of these activities, such as regulating our life with a routine, sitting in a specific posture, controlling our breathing, and focusing our mind on certain things. This is a fraction of all that could be controlled but is currently not in our control. By way of this limited control, we can gain full control over the mind and body. The situation is therefore neither absolute control nor the absence of control. In this post, I will describe why both misconceptions (about control or its absence) arise and why they are wrong. I will then describe how the alternative method of control exists and is used to gain greater control.

The Controller and the Controlled

In Bhagavad-Gita 3.27, Lord Kṛṣṇa states: The spirit soul bewildered by the influence of false ego thinks himself the doer of activities that are in actuality carried out by the three modes of material nature.

Our bodies are not in our control, nor are the senses (of knowing and acting), mind (thoughts), intellect (beliefs), ego (goals), and the moral sense (values). They work automatically like a machine, but it is not a mathematical machine; it is a machine of guna (qualities) and karma (activities) governed by the cosmic law of choice and consequence. We *think* we make choices, but they are mostly made by matter. This leads some to ask: If there is no choice, why are there consequences? The answer is that while matter indeed controls us, it is we who *allow* this control, which makes us responsible for our choices. We could prevent matter from controlling us, but the process of gaining control is harder than allowing it.

Some of you might have seen the British TV series *Yes, Prime Minister*. In it, officially, the power is in the hands of the Prime Minister, but he is in fact being manipulated by the bureaucrats. The bureaucrats instill in the Prime Minister fear of outcomes, scare him with the complexity of the procedures, and thus keep him under their control rather than doing what he wants done. These days, the Prime Minister is called the "state" while the bureaucracy (in some descriptions) is called the "deep state". Officially, the "state" is in control, but unofficially, the "deep state" is in control. People outside the government think that the Prime Minister is making all the decisions that are actually made by the bureaucrats.

This is a good analogy for understanding the relationship between the soul and matter. The soul is the "state" and the body, senses, mind, intellect, ego, and moral sense are the "deep state". From the outside, everyone thinks that the soul makes the choices, but on the inside, the body, senses, mind, intellect, ego, and moral sense control the soul. Just as the Prime Minister, deluded by a false ego, pretends to the public that he controls the government, similarly, deluded by the false ego, the soul pretends to be in control of the body, senses, mind, intellect, ego, and the moral sense. The Prime Minister's speeches are written by a bureaucrat, which the Prime Minister vocalizes to the public. What we hear are the words of the bureaucrats writing the speeches, but the Prime Minister pretends (and the people think) that they are the Prime Minister's thoughts. Similarly, matter controls the soul, who pretends to be in control.

The Abrahamic vs. the Vedic Soul

Thus, in the Vedic tradition, material life is called *bondage,* and exit from this life is called *liberation*. These two concepts are quite different from the Abrahamic concepts of *damnation* and *salvation*. In the Abrahamic description, God damned Adam and Eve to material life and God will deliver salvation. But in the Vedic texts, the soul chose to come to the bondage of material life, and it can choose to attain liberation. Since the soul was not damned to enter the world, bondage is caused by its choices. Since the soul will be liberated by its choices, salvation given by God is not liberation attained by the soul.

The Vedic and the Abrahamic ideas of the soul, world, entry, and exit are opposite. In the Abrahamic story, God gave Adam dominion over the world, so man is fully in control, especially if that man accepts the religious covenant with God. But in the Vedic story, Adam came to this world thinking that he would get dominion over the world, but in actuality, he became a prisoner. To prove that he has dominion over the world, Adam pretends to be in charge of the world, which is periodically disproved by his reality, but still he is unable to give up his desire to be the controller and just tries and fails to get dominion.

Thus, Abrahamic religions talk about how the soul has free will—i.e., control over the body and the world. But the Vedic tradition talks about how the soul is living in bondage—i.e., without control over his life, body, senses, mind, intellect, ego, and the moral sense. Accordingly, Vedic liberation is escaping the prison by giving up the dominating mindset, while Abrahamic redemption is the fulfillment of the dominating mindset by gaining full control over the prison. The fact is that everyone pretending to be in control of the world is already controlled from within by material nature. He is a prisoner of his body and mind, pretending to be the overlord of the world, and hence, in a delusion. Thus, the soul has dominion over matter in Abrahamic religions, and matter has dominion over the soul in the Vedic texts. Abrahamic religions talk about God-given freedoms, and the Vedic tradition talks about self-inflicted bondage.

How Demigods Control the Soul

The body we think is ours is not actually so. Every part of "our" body is a part of some demigod's body, who controls it like we *think* we control our body. Our blood circulation is due to Vāyu, our digestion is controlled by Agni, our mind is influenced by Chandra, and our intellect is under the regulation of Surya. Due to this dominion over every aspect of our life, it is said that the demigods live in our body, like many tenants living in a single house. They control different parts of the house and manipulate the supposed "owner" of the body into thinking that he is in control, while that "owner" is just one of the millions of tenants in the body—by and large, the tenant least in control. We have no privacy, confidentiality, or secrecy. Every moment we are watched, recorded, supervised, and controlled by the demigods.

Vedic astrology reflects this idea of a controlled life. Our life is divided into 12 aspects called houses, each pertaining to a different facet of our life. There are native lords of each house, whose position in the astrological chart decides how, when, and where that aspect rises or falls. As the lord of one house enters another house, it influences the working of the native lord of that house. As the lords of different houses influence each other, our life changes with a minor change in the position of these lords. How is Vedic astrology able to predict terrestrial events based on celestial events? The answer is that our life is controlled by the demigods. Each lord of each house is a demigod ruling over some aspect of our lives. But he or she is not the only controller in the body. Our body is a puppet controlled by many strings.

Decline of the Vedic Understanding

This idea of the heavens controlling the earth was indeed the idea of science in all ancient civilizations. The heavens were plural, organized in a hierarchy, and doing science meant knowing this hierarchy of heavens, along with the aspect of life they held sway over. Almost all ancient cultures that enunciated this idea of science are now gone; only the Vedic tradition still continues. Meanwhile, a materialistic idea of science in which the heavens don't exist, and the earth is controlled by mathematical laws, has replaced the ancient science. In fact, this materialistic ideology calls all ancient civilizations inferior to itself.

This change is the result of two key shifts in thinking. In India, impersonalism claimed that demigods only exist in our minds, and religiously minded men had anthropomorphically projected the orderly workings of the mind and the body into the control of heavenly personalities. In the West, Abrahamic ideologies claimed that demigods were false gods, and the world was controlled by mathematical laws. Thus, both impersonalism and Abrahamic ideologies rejected demigods. Abrahamic ideologies also rejected rebirth and karma, but impersonalists did not. Of course, impersonalists couldn't explain how karma and rebirth work without demigods, so their rejection was devoid of both mathematical laws and the demigods.

This rejection was then picked up in Western psychology by Carl Jung as archetypes. He claimed that ideas of truth, beauty, justice, ideal mother, ideal father, ideal teacher, and ideal ruler were immanent in all minds, and they had historically been projected anthropomorphically into heavenly deities. Jung claimed that the commonalities among deities across ancient civilizations were a side-effect of all minds having the same archetypes, with each civilization projecting them into a heavenly deity. This was Jung's way of rejecting Abrahamic ideologies in which the human mind (or the soul) is sinful by birth, and that truth, beauty, and justice could only be known through a revelation given by a messiah. Jung was inspired into his archetype theory after reading the works of the impersonalists in India. He outlined a path in which one could reject revelatory religions and pursue truth, beauty, and justice within ourselves.

The Emergence of False Ideologies

And thus, impersonalism in India, Abrahamic ideologies all over the world, and more recently, Jungian archetypes, produced the false idea that we are in control of our minds and bodies. It goes against the discoveries of neuroscience (that we will discuss later in this article) and of practical realization, in which we are not free, making it an anti-science and anti-commonsense worldview. The currently suggested resolution out of that discovery is that we are living in a simulation, and notions of good or bad exist in us to the extent that the simulation shows us those things. And yet, nobody really knows how to escape the simulation. The centuries of talk about man being free have now ended in man living in bondage.

Impersonalism and Jungian archetypes depersonalized demigods into ideas, while Abrahamic ideologies rejected them completely. After that rejection, they are left either with mathematical determinism or, worse, mathematical indeterminism. Under determinism, you have no choice, but at least your life is ordered. Under indeterminism, life isn't even ordered, and you can't blame the chaos on anything. In this chaos, New Age religions following impersonalism and Jungian archetypes talk about order created by the human mind. Consciousness and free will are now the gods of the gaps created by science.

The problem is that everyone doesn't have the same idea of truth, beauty, and justice, so there is no basis in saying these ideas are equally and pervasively immanent in all minds. The commonality across ancient civilizations existed when demigods were factually present in the heavens, although partially understood by different cultures. After the Abrahamic religions rejected these demigods, each of them came up with their own covenant under which different ideas of truth, beauty, and justice were upheld by them. These ideologies then went to war with each other because they couldn't prove that their ideas of truth, beauty, and justice were factually correct. The fact is that different covenants were created by different minds with different ideas of truth, beauty, and justice. If they could not reconcile their ideas in the many intervening centuries, what is the basis of thinking that it will happen in the future?

A Semantic Description of Matter

The Vedic texts provide an alternative. The demigods are not just our ideas and ideals. They are persons living in the heavens. And yet, they live both inside and outside our bodies and minds, because their body is idea-like, not substance-like. The perfect form of truth, beauty, and justice lives in another world, and their imperfect forms may exist within our minds. However, the perfect reigns over the imperfect, to bring the imperfection to perfection. Thus, we are not free to anoint our imperfect truth, beauty, and justice to the perfect truth, beauty, and justice—as the liberal conception of the world claims. The real question is, how does something exist both inside and outside, as partial and complete perfection?

Answering that question requires us to rethink matter as ideas. The perfect form of the idea exists outside us, and either perfect or imperfect forms of the same idea may exist within us. As the imperfect is a part of the perfect, hence, we are all part of perfection. And yet, we are not free because the idea exists in us in an imperfect form. We are neither fully enlightened nor completely ignorant. Our freedom depends on the extent to which we are enlightened. If we remain ignorant, we also remain unfree.

If a person's body is conceptualized materially, the demigod must always be outside. If a demigod is depersonalized as an idea, the demigod must exist only in a mind. However, if the demigod's body is an idea, then it can exist both inside and outside, and what is inside is controlled by what is outside. This alternative is presented in the Vedic texts as the philosophy of guna or qualities. Each demigod embodies a particular quality in perfection. The same qualities exist partially and imperfectly in us. The imperfect is a part of the perfect, and the imperfect is controlled by the perfect. The whole doesn't reduce to its parts because many imperfect things don't automatically aggregate into a perfect thing. Those parts have to be organized in a specific way for them to be perfect, which is done by a perfect person. Thus, the world is organized by persons, not ideas. Even ideas live in a person, not in some imaginary idea-world.

Semantics Through an Analogy

The situation could be analogized as many mirrors reflecting a reality—the reality is both inside and outside the mirror, but each mirror sees a part of that reality, and the image within the mirror cannot be equated to reality outside it. Instead, changes to reality change the reflection, and so, the reality controls the reflection.

Thus, the mind is described as a (clean or unclean) mirror in the Vedic texts. However, this is an imperfect analogy because even as one mirror is reflected in other mirrors, the mirrors don't control each other; the reflection is controlled, but the mirror is not. Thereby, if we treated ourselves as mirrors and the demigods as reality, we could not explain how they control us through a reflection.

Therefore, we have to say that the mirror, the reality, and the reflection are all ideas. Then, there are distinct entities, but they are also within each other. A perfect embodiment of some quality resides in heaven, and imperfect embodiments of those qualities exist on earth. Moreover, the perfect controls the imperfect because the imperfect is a part of the perfect, and the perfect holds sway over the imperfect. And thus, the perfect is free while the imperfect is controlled. Even if we cannot see the perfect outside, we aren't free because that whole exists within each part since the whole and the part are ideas.

For instance, the idea color exists inside all shades, such as yellow, red, and blue, and yet, the shades don't exhaust the idea color, and so, the idea is both inside and outside. Each shade is an incomplete and imperfect representation of color, and yet, each shade is a part of the complete and perfect. Thus, even if someone doesn't see a demigod, he can still know that he doesn't control his mind or body. He has to now find an explanation of how and why his mind and body work against his volitional control.

The Necessity of the Demigods

Demigods can't be reduced to ideas (as in impersonalism, Jungian psychology, or a liberal conception of the world). Demigods can't be rejected (as in Abrahamic ideologies). They are persons that exist both inside and outside because their bodies are ideas. The hands of truth, beauty, and justice control parts of truth, beauty, and justice. By the legs, the truth, beauty, and justice come and go. Through the eyes, the whole truth, beauty, and justice see their parts. Through the power of speech, truth, beauty, and justice express their nature. To know truth, beauty, and justice, we have to know how they control, move, see, and express. The capacities of truth, beauty, and justice are just like those in our body. Hence, when we speak of demigods, we are not anthropomorphically projecting what only exists in our minds. We are rather expressing a complete understanding of all that knowing truth, beauty, and justice entail.

And yet, the body of a demigod is not like our body because it is the form of some idea, such as truth, beauty, or justice. That idea is the essence of their mind, from which a body is expanded to hear, touch, see, taste, smell, hold, move, express, and reproduce that idea. Even our bodies are produced from our minds, but our minds are impure. As our mind is filled with lies, injustice, and ugliness, the body becomes more different from a demigod body. The fact that our body appears to have the same shape as that of the demigod body doesn't mean they are the same type; the type is decided by the ideas in the mind, not by the shape of the body. Even demons can have the same bodily shape as ours. They are not human, even as they seem to have a human shape, because a person's type is decided by the mind. Likewise, even God can appear in an animal shape; He is not an animal since the type is given by the mind.

To know the mind, we have to know the activities of all the senses because the mind expresses itself through these senses. Someone can lie through speech, but their actions reveal their true intentions. Someone can speak harshly for a moment, but their kind actions reveal their mind. Thus, a demon or a demigod is not decided by one activity; we have to get a comprehensive understanding. We don't anthropomorphically project good and evil in us as demigods and demons in the overworld or the underworld; instead, we know them by the type of their minds. Whatever good or evil exists partially in us, it exists in a purer and concentrated form in demigods and demons. They are the versions of "purer good" and "purer evil".

The Rise of the Demonic Mindset

However, when truth, beauty, and justice were depersonalized as ideas by the Greeks, they became deaf, dumb, and blind. Ideas became static and impotent fixtures in an imaginary Platonic

World with no influence on the present world. In fact, the Sophists claimed that *Man is the measure of all things*, which means he is free to define the meaning of truth, beauty, and justice. Greeks effectively transferred the power of demigods into the hands of mankind. From the denial of demigods and their replacement by humanity stemmed Abrahamic religions, Western philosophy, and modern science. They have lived under the delusion of mankind's prowess to define their own truth, beauty, and justice, and they keep inventing new religions, philosophies, and scientific theories under the belief that mankind is free to speculate and invent truth, beauty, and justice. That supposed freedom is based on the denial of the actual controllers of the world, and hence, the whole enterprise is just an elaborate delusion.

In fact, since demons try to deny and destroy the demigods, the denial of demigods in philosophy, religion, and science is indeed the demonic mindset. It spreads in society via the ramparts of religious, educational, political, economic, and social institutions. We can see the effects of that demonic mindset in the centuries of killing of nature, animals, humans, cultures, and civilizations that were earlier living in harmony. Indeed, the Vedic texts talk about how the world is a family. But we can't have a family in which some members kill other members to get exclusive dominion. Those who can't read the mind and just see the body can't understand that demons and demigods cannot be family. They may foolishly talk about making a family of demons and demigods, but they can never succeed. Their foolishness is trying to define a person based on their bodily shape rather than their mental ideas.

Choice is Acceptance and Rejection

With the semantic view of matter, we can understand that we are neither fully in control nor absolutely without control. Our body is a part of other bodies that we don't see, and yet, we are still one of the tenants in the body. We falsely claim to be fully in control, like the Prime Minister pretends to hold power. The bureaucrats don't want to be in the limelight. They like to control everything, but they want the Prime Minister to take responsibility. Thus, the job of the bureaucrat is permanent, but that of the

Prime Minister is temporary. The bureaucrat gets the best of both worlds—job security and total control without any responsibility. The responsibility of the bureaucrat's choices is transferred to the Prime Minister. Similarly, the demigods control our lives, but transfer the responsibility of their control to us.

That is because we are fools to want to be the Prime Minister. We work hard to get elected, then we are controlled, and finally we are blamed. Meanwhile, the actual controller remains unaccountable and invisible. The material world is the delusion of wanting to be in control, being misled by the actual controller, and then suffering the consequences of being misled. Factually, everyone is misled in the way they want to be misled. If a Prime Minister wants to be flattered, the bureaucracy flatters him. That is the way the bureaucracy sustains its grip on power. Similarly, the way the demigods mislead a person is the way that person wants to be misled. To get out of this deception, one has to reject the proposals of the bureaucrats and compel them to make a new proposal. In so doing, he could regain control.

The Prime Minister's power lies in selective *rejection* and *acceptance.* The Prime Minister loses power if he always accepts the proposals from the bureaucrats. To gain power, he must sometimes reject their proposals. The Prime Minister is not expected to do the job of the bureaucrats. But he has to make the bureaucrats do their job as per his wishes. They are interdependent realities, and yet, the Prime Minister holds power over the bureaucrats. That power doesn't mean the bureaucrats are mindless machines, nor does it mean that the Prime Minister is a mindless machine. Exactly like that, neither the soul nor the mind-body is a mindless machine. They are just like the Prime Minister and the bureaucrats.

The mind says: "Do this," and the soul mostly acquiesces—"Yes, of course". To gain control over the mind, the soul has to sometimes say, "No, of course not". Then the mind will make another proposal, and the soul could potentially accept that. Thus, there is a power of choice which is exercised by rejecting what the mind says. If the soul always *accepts* the mind's dictations, the power of choice is not used.

And yet, since the soul has the power of choice, not using the power is also a choice. The Prime Minister, controlled by the bureaucrats, chooses to remain weak, subservient, and obedient. He was not elected to his role to do so. But if the Prime Minister doesn't exercise his power of choice, that itself constitutes a choice, after which the Prime Minister (and not the bureaucrat) is responsible even for things that the bureaucrat may have done based on the Prime Minister's approval, acquiescence, or compliance.

Going against the bureaucracy is hard because the bureaucracy always plays with the Prime Minister's fears, anxieties, ignorance, hopes, and desires. The bureaucracy makes the Prime Minister think that it is working in the Prime Minister's interest, when it is only working in its own interest of sustaining its stronghold over the power centers. Similarly, going against the wishes, demands, and whims of the body and mind is very hard. But if we accept these whims, we are in bondage. Liberation means we can go against these whims. Thus, liberation is incredibly hard. At every moment, the body and mind will show their wishes, demands, and whims. If we accept, we are bound; if we reject, we are liberated.

The Working of Consciousness

Acceptance and rejection operate by consciousness moving inward and outward. Consciousness moves inward during sleep, and it moves outward during waking. The choice of consciousness exists as inward and outward movement (there are actually five kinds of movement—upward, downward, inward, outward, and around, but we will restrict ourselves to just two to keep the discussion simple).

New Age impersonalists talk about a consciousness without will because their idea of consciousness is wakefulness. However, yogic traditions talk about yoga-nidra, the yogic sleep, in which a person is awake from a first-person viewpoint and asleep from a third-person viewpoint. A person sitting in a class, but staring into the blank, is said to be sleeping or daydreaming by the teacher because waking is not really waking if we don't pay attention to the reality entailed by waking. If we are lost in our imaginary world, we are dreaming while waking. If our minds remain blank while waking, we are actually sleeping.

Consciousness is never devoid of will because it moves, which is called *attention*. We move our attention from one thing to another, attending to different sensations, thoughts, judgments, and emotions. Even while eating food, our consciousness moves between taste, touch, smell, and sight. Within sight, it moves between color, shape, and size. Within touch, it moves between hardness, heat, and roughness. The consciousness is always moving, never static. And yet, unlike the physicalist conception of matter, it can control its own movement. The movement and the ability to control it constitute will. Denying the will to consciousness is simply ignorance of what consciousness is. Just because the denial is common these days doesn't mean it is true. Every person can introspect and understand why the claim is false.

The acceptance of the mind is consciousness moving outward and attaching itself to the thoughts created by the mind. The rejection of the mind is consciousness moving inward and detaching itself from the thoughts created by the mind. Since consciousness can attach or detach, there is a power of choice. If we learn to control our conscious movement, we gain power over matter, because regardless of what the mind or the body says, consciousness can withdraw and not listen to what they are saying.

Here is an experiment everyone can do with themselves—withdraw from a thought, and you will find that the thought disappears. If you had stayed with the thought, it might have developed into an action. But if you withdraw from the thought, the thought disappears, and the action never appears. Thus, the power of will is the inward and outward movement of consciousness. We always hold sway over the mind and body if we know how to withdraw. That doesn't mean we can always control what the mind or the body is doing, but it means that we will not be aware and responsible for those actions.

Benjamin Libet's Experiments

The principle of choice as rejection was proven by Benjamin Libet in neuroscience experiments when he showed that the brain creates a proposal several milliseconds before the person reports accepting it. Under the Abrahamic concept of free will—i.e., the soul having dominion over matter—a person must report having an idea before it is measured in the brain. Since the opposite was observed, most people interpreted it to mean that the soul has no free will. But Benjamin Libet clarified that we don't have *free will,* although we have *free won't,* which means the (rarely used) power of rejecting the proposals. We are compliant, subservient, and obedient to the proposals made by the body and the mind, so it seems we have no choice. But the power of choice exists as the capacity to reject the mind-body proposals.

Libet's experiments pose challenges to the Abrahamic conception of soul and matter, under which the soul controls matter, because they show that our brain produces thoughts before the conscious person becomes aware of them. They pose no challenges to the Vedic conception of soul and matter under which matter controls the soul and matter proposes to the soul which the soul mostly accepts, although in principle, it could also have rejected by withdrawing from that proposal. Therefore, the experimental denial of the Abrahamic conception of free will is not the denial of the Vedic conception of free will. Instead, the experiment proves the basic fact that we are living in bondage rather than freedom.

The Vedic Realization of the Self

Once the basic fact about our bondage is confirmed empirically (through introspection or experiment), we can move toward understanding the spiritual path. The Vedic tradition always teaches how to control the body and mind by rejecting their urges, demands, and proposals. That is called *tapa* or austerity. The mind-body scream—"I can't live without this!". But the sober person says—"Sure, you can; you are living as long as I (the soul) am with you". By rejecting the demands of the mind-body, they are toughened. They don't scream as much as before. Over time, they become silent. They know there is no point in screaming to one who doesn't listen. This sobriety is called *dhīra,* and the disturbance after the mind-body screaming is called *adhīra.* Almost everyone at present is *adhīra,* but through gradual practice, everyone can become *dhīra.* Becoming sober instead of disturbed is a basic goal of spiritual practice.

Everyone who claims to have free will doesn't have willpower, which means the capacity to reject the mind-body screams. The mind screams, "Do this!" and we say, "Of course, what choice do I have?" And out of false pride, we say, "I chose to do this," although deep inside we know we are not in control. We are slaves, puppets, and prisoners of the mind-body, but we pretend to be the masters. The real mastery is to gain control over the mind-body. Before you conquer the world, try to conquer your mind-body. One who has gained this mastery becomes peaceful, satisfied, calm, equipoised, and contented.

Śrīmad Bhagavatam 1.2.21 states: Thus, the knot in the heart is pierced, and all misgivings are cut to pieces. The chain of fruitive actions is terminated when one sees the self as master. The Sanskrit words are dṛṣṭa evātmanīśvare, which means always seeing oneself as the lord of the mind-body. It comes after a long time, which means we become the lord by practice, although we are not the lord right now.

Many people say that we are Brahman, although they cannot tolerate the screaming of the mind and body. We are indeed Brahman and superior to matter, but we have forgotten what we are, and this remembrance has to be attained through practice. In that state, one becomes free of distress, fear, and death. I am the lord, so I will do as I please, which means I will choose whether to be in the body, leave the body, or which body to go to next. The body doesn't control me. I control the body. If the body screams, I will just leave it for another body.

The Vedic Realization of God

This is liberation, self-realization, or self-mastery. It is the beginning of spiritual understanding. As one realizes how he is free of lust, anger, greed, pride, envy, and confusion, he realizes the true nature of the self, and then he slowly realizes the true nature of God, in analogy to himself, i.e., free of lust, anger, greed, pride, envy, and confusion. Without self-realization, there can be no God realization. Instead, those under lust, anger, greed, pride, envy, and confusion impute these attributes to God. For example, they hypothesize that just as they are envious of others, God must be envious of other gods. They postulate that just because they have lust and greed for worship, so God must be lusty and greedy for worship. The religion created by a soul under material bondage always increases material bondage, which means one following it becomes more lusty, greedy, angry, proud, envious, and confused.

God is always happy in Himself, but He wants the pleasure of living with other self-satisfied individuals. That is because happiness and pleasure are not the same thing. Happiness is about what we are, and pleasure is about what we have. Happiness depends on the self, while pleasure depends on others. When we are happy with ourselves, we don't need others. We may interact with them for their benefit, but it is not long-lasting. The eternally lasting interaction is when others are also self-satisfied.

The self-satisfied person serves others, while the self-dissatisfied person dominates others. Those who try to dominate the world are unhappy with themselves. They try to compensate for their unhappiness with pleasure. However, those who serve are served, and those who dominate are dominated. By associating with the self-satisfied, we learn the meaning of self-satisfaction—i.e., being happy with who we are, relishing our own existence, and working for others' benefit. If we can become self-satisfied, then we can understand God—happy with Himself, relishing His own existence, and working for the benefit of others. Without the association of the self-satisfied, there is neither self-realization nor God-realization. Instead, one projects his ideas of imperfection onto the self-realized and God-realized personalities, but because he remains self-dissatisfied, his projections also keep changing, which is called evolving religions.

Prescription for a Degraded Age

In this age, we cannot control our minds and bodies. We can't even fathom the meaning of yoga-nidra, or awake from the first-person viewpoint and asleep from the third-person viewpoint. Hence, it is advised that we become a selfless servant of God through His selfless servants. Some might say that we don't know a selfless servant of God, so how can we become a selfless servant of God? The answer is that when we sincerely want to become a selfless servant of God, we automatically find other selfless servants of God who teach us how to become a selfless servant of God. We have to show the inclination and desire to be a selfless servant of God before we will find other selfless servants in proportion to our selflessness.

We prefer what we are. Hence, if we are selfless, we prefer those who are selfless. Then the vision of the selfless servants of God also comes automatically. In proportion to our selflessness, a genuine person automatically comes into our life, and we recognize that person as genuine because we are genuine. If we are fakers, the mind prefers a faker just like oneself, and is misled by the fakery. Therefore, change in the self is always the cause of lasting change in our world. The change in the world is seldom, if ever, a cause of the change in the self because we reject changes in the world contrary to our own nature.

To bring that change in the self, we have to understand how we are living in bondage, how that bondage is controlled, what real freedom is, how to attain that freedom, and the state of the individual living in that freedom. In short, everything begins with education. Without education, there are a million false alternatives, but none of those persist. Or, they simply pretend to persist by continuously evolving and modifying themselves. They were self-dissatisfied before, and they will be self-dissatisfied after.

But if one finds a selfless servant of God, he must become a selfless servant of that servant. In that mood of servitude, one humbly associates with the selfless servant and understands how he is self-satisfied, and by analogy, how God is self-satisfied. By service, the selfless servant of God reveals to his servant the nature of God. It is not a theoretical idea; it is practically seen in the teacher's day-to-day life. Thus, it is said that by the grace of such devotees, God is known, and without the grace of such devotees, God is never known. The yogic process of self-mastery is very hard. But someone else can lift us, if we agree to be controlled by them. The choice is either to be controlled by a servant of God or to be controlled by the mind and the body. There is no freedom, as a fool imagines. The choice is to serve the servant of God, or stay in bondage of the mind and body. God and His servants are not interested in the so-called freedom-loving self-serving individuals. They can figure out their life's problems on their own. If one wants to be lifted from their condition, they have to selflessly serve the selfless servants of God.

Liberation Can't Deny Demigods

There are misconceptions about the role of demigods for the liberated person, too, perpetuated by the impersonalists. They claim that for a liberated person, the demigods are simply illusions. This false claim never explains how our bodies and minds were working while we were in bondage, so they have no clue how they keep working after we are liberated. The fact is that the demigods never give up control over the body. However, their reign over our mind-body can be serving or dominating. The demigods serve the self-satisfied and dominate the self-dissatisfied. The reign of the demigods is neither good nor bad by itself. It depends on whether that control serves or dominates the soul. Demigods can do both.

Those who serve God selflessly are served by the demigods because they, too, are servants of God. The mind-body of a pure servant of God is his servant. The pure servant of God doesn't feel oppressed by his body and mind because the demigods are serving rather than dominating him. Therefore, it appears that the pure servant of God has conquered his body and mind. But it is not a conquest because the mind-body still works under the control of demigods, who are empowered to control the body and the mind. And yet, because the demigods become his servants rather than masters, it appears that the devotee of God has conquered the mind and body. The devotees of God realize free will, i.e., absolute autonomy over the mind and body. And yet, they are never proud of their achievement. Others, who try to gain control over the mind and the body, are always in a battle against demigod control. They sometimes gain control, and that makes them proud, which often becomes the cause of their eventual downfall.

Most people who talk about yoga at present think that they will gain mastery over their mind and body. They don't know that their supposed mastery means the subservience of the more powerful demigods. Why would a more powerful person become subservient? There is one answer—the person becomes an unalloyed devotee of God. And thus, yogic mastery is attained only by the servants of God. Everyone else pretending to control the mind-body is fighting a losing battle. They have no idea how powerless they are in contrast to demigods. Impersonalism, Abrahamic ideologies, and Jungian psychology have made them believe that they can be masters of their mind and body, or that they are the only tenant living in the mind-body, although they cannot explain how this mind-body works without their intervention.

Free Will is a Difficult Subject

Thus, the question of free will is quite involved. It begins by realizing that we have almost no control over the mind-body, and it culminates in the realization that the only way to gain that control is to become a pure servant of God. The former is bondage and the latter is liberation. There is no damnation or salvation. Freedom is not a birthright. In fact, almost everyone at present is born a slave, lives as a slave, and dies a slave, unless he becomes a devotee of God. The slave thinks that his freedom means others' slavery because he has no idea about real freedom. The slave invents fictions about being born free, endowed with God-given rights, while he spends his life denying the same fictions and rights for others. The true devotees of God have no business with these man-made fictions or their lifelong denials. They begin by teaching how everyone is a slave and then enunciate the path of freedom by serving God.

All these ideas were quite well-known earlier. The present confusion on free will is created by Abrahamic religions, Western philosophy, and modern science, under which man is born free to rule the world. Thus, free will means man controlling nature, animals, and other men. Then the impersonalists imagine that they can get out of this controlling mindset through renunciation, but they have no way to lift themselves. The formerly practiced yogic processes are too hard for this age. And yet, they imagine that by philosophy and yoga, they will attain liberation. Their failure is entailed by the preeminence of the demigods over the mind and body, and by their rejection of the selfless servants of God as people living in the delusion of giving the formless a definite form. Then there are New Age religions in which truth, beauty, and justice exist within us, and everyone is free to create their own version of these. Some New Age religions try to separate consciousness from free will; for them, consciousness means observation, including of will, as will is not a basic trait of each person. They think that they shall become free of the mind and body bondage simply by observing how they are working. Their failure is entailed by the fact that if we keep observing, the consciousness is sucked into the observed, and comes under its control. Finally, there is materialism in which nature is governed by deterministic laws, and if these deterministic laws prove inadequate, then nature must be random. Either way, we can't do anything about it. It's very hard to count all the misconceptions.

Undoing all these misconceptions is hard, but it can be done by each individual undertaking a deep study of the central problem of life, namely, that we are living in bondage of the mind and body. Instead, most people spend their time perpetuating the bondage by obediently serving the mind and body, or thinking that they were born to rule the world, or that they will get out of bondage by some bodily exercises, or that they will attain liberation simply by observing the bondage, or if these are not possible, life must be lived helplessly under material control. Ignorance is the root of all bondage; we believe in falsehoods, and that perpetuates the bondage. It is not that knowledge is impossible. It is just that we perpetuate our bondage by rejecting or neglecting the process of knowledge.

www.ingramcontent.com/pod-product-compliance
Ingram Content Group UK Ltd.
Pitfield, Milton Keynes, MK11 3LW, UK
UKHW041313190726
13845UKWH00025B/234

9 789385 384462